The Agnostic Trader

Exploring the Financial Markets using Python and Machine Learning

David López Oñate

Contents

Purpose of the Book

In today's rapidly evolving financial markets, automation and artificial intelligence have moved from being a novelty to becoming a core component of successful trading strategies. Automation allows traders to execute with precision and discipline, while machine learning equips them with predictive capabilities that human intuition alone cannot achieve. This book, *The Principled Trader*, aims to bridge the gap between these cutting-edge technologies and practical, robust trading strategies. It offers a step-by-step guide for creating an automated trading system using Python and Machine Learning, implemented within the powerful MetaTrader 5 platform.

The core mission of this book is to demystify the process of developing data-driven trading systems, making it accessible to traders, data scientists, developers, and financial enthusiasts alike. Whether you are a professional trader looking to systematize your approach, a developer seeking to leverage the power of AI in finance, or a beginner intrigued by this intersection, this book provides a clear and structured pathway to developing a sophisticated trading framework that can navigate the complex, high-speed world of modern financial markets.

Why a Principled, Evidence-Based Approach?

The philosophy that underpins this book is that of a **principled, data-driven methodology**. In financial markets, where uncertainty reigns and conditions change at a moment's notice, relying on rigid assumptions, a single favorite strategy, or pre-defined rules can be a fragile approach.

Instead, this book champions a methodology that is **agnostic about outcomes but rigorous in its process**. We do not begin with a preconceived bias about which model, feature set, or market condition will yield the best results. Instead, we construct a disciplined, multi-stage pipeline to systematically test our hypotheses. The final strategy is chosen not based on dogma or intuition, but on the basis of robust, cross-validated evidence.

This approach acknowledges the inherent unpredictability of markets and embraces the idea that no single strategy is universally effective. By remaining open to multiple models and features—and letting hard evidence dictate the best combinations—the trader becomes more adaptive and resilient. This disciplined adaptability is crucial for long-term success.

Scope of the Book

The scope of this book is highly practical. While theoretical foundations are covered to ensure a firm understanding of the concepts, the primary focus is on hands-on implementation. You will learn how to build a complete, end-to-end pipeline to discover, validate, and deploy machine learning models that drive trading decisions.

Throughout the chapters, you will be guided through the following core phases:

- **Financial Data Processing:** Learn how to gather, clean, and preprocess historical market data, transforming it into the high-quality features required for model training. This includes the use of technical indicators, price data, and volatility measures.

- **A Robust Framework for Building Predictive Models:** You will explore a disciplined, four-stage pipeline for model development. This is the core of the book. Instead of a chaotic search, you will learn how to:

  1. Select a strong **Base Set** of features using statistical methods.

  2. Conduct a **"Model Horse Race"** to identify the most promising model architectures.

  3. **Fine-tune** the top models by optimizing their hyperparameters with GridSearchCV.

  4. Produce a single, **champion model** that has survived this rigorous validation gauntlet.

- **Honest Backtesting and Performance Analysis:** A significant portion of this book is dedicated to the proper evaluation of trading strategies. You will learn how to backtest your champion model on unseen historical data, assess key performance metrics, and avoid critical pitfalls like overfitting. We will explore how to analyze performance in detail, including separating results for BUY and SELL trades to understand a model's specific strengths.

- **Live Trading Implementation:** You will learn how to operationalize your validated model in a real-time trading environment using Python and MetaTrader 5. This includes practical guides on executing trades, setting data-driven stop-loss and take-profit levels, and managing open positions.

- **Continuous Model Improvement:** As markets evolve, so must our strategies. You will learn the importance of monitoring live performance and the necessity of periodically retraining models to ensure they remain adapted to current market conditions.

A Comprehensive, Adaptive Trading System

The ultimate purpose of this book is to empower you to build a fully automated trading **framework** that is profitable, adaptive, and principled in its approach. By the end of this journey, you will have:

- A deep understanding of how to apply a robust machine learning workflow to financial markets.

- The ability to integrate Python-driven models into MetaTrader 5 for live trading.

- Practical skills in developing, backtesting, and optimizing algorithmic trading strategies.

- The knowledge to build a system that can be continually adapted to changing market conditions.

Ultimately, the successful quantitative trader understands that flexibility and adaptability—guided by a disciplined and evidence-based process—are the keys to success. This book is designed to provide you with the tools, knowledge, and mindset to thrive in a world where data, machine learning, and adaptability converge to unlock new possibilities.

Who This Book Is For

The Agnostic Trader is written for a diverse audience, including:

- **Traders and Investors** aiming to enhance and automate their strategies with a data-driven edge.

- **Python Developers** interested in applying their programming skills to the exciting domain of financial markets.

- **Data Scientists and Machine Learning Practitioners** looking to apply their expertise to the unique challenges of financial time-series forecasting.

- **Financial Analysts and Quants** who want to complement traditional financial models with modern machine learning techniques.

The book assumes only a basic familiarity with Python and general financial market concepts. All machine learning techniques are explained within the context of our practical framework, making the content accessible even to those new to the field.

Why Python and MetaTrader 5?

The decision to combine Python and MetaTrader 5 is a strategic one. **Python** is the undisputed language of data science and machine learning, offering a vast ecosystem of powerful libraries (scikit-learn, pandas, XGBoost). **MetaTrader 5** is one of the most robust and widely used platforms for retail and institutional traders, providing reliable real-time data and execution.

The synergy of these two tools creates an unparalleled framework. It allows us to perform complex, computationally intensive research and model development in Python, and then seamlessly deploy those models into a world-class trading environment for live execution. This book will guide you through harnessing the combined power of both platforms to build cutting-edge algorithmic trading systems.

Chapter 1: What is Algorithmic Trading?

Algorithmic trading, often referred to as algo trading or automated trading, represents a transformative shift in the way financial markets operate. It involves the use of computer programs, designed to follow predefined rules and statistical models, to execute trading decisions automatically. These algorithms evaluate market conditions by analyzing factors such as price movements, volatility, and volume, allowing them to make split-second buy or sell decisions without the need for human intervention. In doing so, algorithmic trading enhances the speed, precision, and discipline of trading, offering a distinct advantage in modern financial markets.

At its core, algorithmic trading enables market participants to exploit the processing power of computers to execute strategies more efficiently than any human could. It's a practice increasingly employed by institutional investors, hedge funds, and sophisticated retail traders. This book will guide you through the process of building your own powerful, machine learning-driven algorithmic trading system.

1.1 The Advantages of an Algorithmic Approach

Algorithmic trading offers several distinct advantages over manual trading, extending beyond mere efficiency to include emotional discipline and the ability to test strategies with scientific rigor.

- **Speed and Efficiency:** Algorithms can process vast amounts of market data and execute trades almost instantly. In today's fast-moving markets, where milliseconds matter, this speed provides a critical edge, allowing strategies to capitalize on fleeting opportunities that are invisible to the manual trader.

- **Emotion-Free Trading:** Human traders are subject to emotional biases—fear, greed, and hope—that can lead to irrational and costly decisions. An algorithm operates without any emotional interference. By adhering strictly to its programming, it executes the intended strategy with perfect discipline, even in the most volatile and stressful market conditions.

- **Consistency and Precision:** An automated system operates with unwavering consistency. It follows its rules with precision, executing trades at the exact moments dictated by the strategy, 24 hours a day, without fatigue or error. This ensures that no valid trading opportunity is missed due to inattention or human error.

- **Backtesting and Optimization:** A major advantage is the ability to perform rigorous **backtesting**. Before risking any real capital, a strategy can be tested on years of historical data to evaluate how it would have performed. This process is essential for refining parameters, understanding a strategy's risk profile, and building confidence in its efficacy.

1.2 The Inherent Challenges and Risks

While compelling, the benefits of algorithmic trading are accompanied by significant challenges that must be respected. A successful algorithmic trader is not just a programmer but also a vigilant risk manager.

- **Overfitting and Curve-Fitting:** This is the greatest pitfall in quantitative trading. It is the dangerous temptation to fine-tune an algorithm so that it performs perfectly on *past* data. A strategy that is over-optimized has not learned a true market edge; it has merely "memorized" the historical noise. Such a strategy is fragile and almost certain to fail in live market conditions.

- **Market Complexity and Unpredictability:** Financial markets are not static systems. They are complex, adaptive, and subject to sudden regime shifts driven by unpredictable geopolitical and macroeconomic events. An algorithm trained on data from a low-volatility trending market may fail catastrophically when a market crash occurs.

- **Technical and Infrastructure Risks:** An automated system is dependent on technology. Network outages, server failures, data feed errors, or bugs in the code can all lead to significant losses. Robust infrastructure and continuous monitoring are not optional; they are essential.

1.3 The Methodology of This Book: The Agnostic Trader

Many books on algorithmic trading present a collection of pre-defined strategies. This book takes a different approach. We will not just give you a set of rules to follow; we will teach you how to build a **"model factory"**—a complete, end-to-end pipeline for discovering, validating, and deploying your own unique, data-driven strategies.

Our core philosophy is that of the **Agnostic Trader**. This approach is "agnostic" in that it makes no preconceived assumptions about which model or feature will work best. Instead, it trusts a **rigorous, evidence-based process** to guide us to the most robust solution. This book will guide you, step-by-step, through building this four-stage pipeline:

1. **Principled Feature Selection:** We begin by using statistical methods to distill a large pool of indicators into a small, powerful "Base Set" of features that are both relevant and non-redundant.

2. **Competitive Model Evaluation:** We conduct a "horse race," pitting a diverse roster of machine learning models against each other in a fair, cross-validated competition to see which architectural family is best suited for the data.

3. **Focused Hyperparameter Tuning:** We take only the winning models and conduct a "deep dive," using sophisticated tuning techniques like GridSearchCV to optimize their internal settings for peak performance.

4. **Honest Out-of-Sample Validation:** The final champion model is subjected to a strict final exam—a backtest on completely unseen data—to provide an unbiased estimate of its real-world potential.

By following this structured methodology, we directly combat the primary risks of algorithmic trading, especially overfitting. We build a system where the final model is chosen not by luck or by bias, but because it has survived a demanding gauntlet of statistical validation.

1.4 The Strategic Focus: Short-Term, Data-Driven Models

This book concentrates on **short-term trading strategies**, where positions are typically held for a few hours to a few days. This focus is deliberate, as this style of trading is uniquely suited to the strengths of a machine learning-driven algorithmic approach.

- **Maximizing Opportunities:** Short-term timeframes offer a higher frequency of trading signals, providing more opportunities for a model to apply its statistical edge.

- **Reduced Overnight Risk:** By often closing positions within the same day or a few days, we limit our exposure to unpredictable events that can occur when markets are closed.

- **Alignment with Machine Learning:** Short-term data is rich and voluminous, providing the vast amount of information that machine learning algorithms need to detect subtle patterns and relationships.

We will explore common trading archetypes like **trend-following**, **mean-reversion**, and **breakout** strategies, not as manually coded rule sets, but as the types of market behavior our machine learning models will learn to identify automatically.

1.5 Conclusion: Your Journey as an Agnostic Systems Architect

This book is designed for a diverse audience, from experienced traders seeking to automate their strategies, to data scientists and developers looking to apply their skills in the exciting domain of financial markets. It assumes only a basic familiarity with Python and financial markets, guiding you through every necessary concept.

The journey ahead is not simply about writing code to buy and sell. It is about learning the discipline of a quantitative researcher and the skills of a systems architect. You will learn to build, test, and manage a sophisticated ecosystem that transforms raw data into intelligent, automated trading decisions. Welcome to the world of the agnostic, data-driven trading.

Chapter 2: An Introduction to Machine Learning for Trading

2.1 From Human Rules to Machine Learning

Machine Learning (ML) is a transformative branch of artificial intelligence (AI) that empowers computers to learn from data and identify patterns without being explicitly programmed for every possible scenario. This capability has revolutionized modern finance. In a domain as complex and dynamic as the financial markets, machine learning provides a sophisticated framework for moving beyond static, rule-based trading into a world of adaptive, data-driven strategies.

Traditional algorithmic trading often relies on a fixed set of human-defined rules (e.g., "buy when the 50-day moving average crosses above the 200-day"). While effective in certain conditions, these systems are brittle; they cannot adapt when market dynamics change. Machine learning addresses this limitation. An ML model can analyze vast amounts of historical data to learn the subtle, non-linear relationships between market indicators and future price movements.

The primary focus of this book is on a specific, powerful application of ML: **Supervised Classification**. Our goal is not to predict the exact price of an asset tomorrow (a regression task), but to answer a more robust, binary question: "Is the price more likely to go up or down in the next period?" By framing the problem this way, we can build models that provide clear, actionable trading signals.

2.2 The Core Paradigm: Supervised Learning

The methodology in this book is built entirely on supervised learning. The concept is analogous to a student studying for an exam with a book of practice problems that includes the correct answers.

1. **The Data (The "Practice Problems"):** We provide the model with a large historical dataset. Each row in the dataset is a "problem."

2. **The Features (X):** For each problem, we provide a set of clues. In our case, these are the values of technical indicators at a specific point in time (e.g., CCI = 150, ADX = 45).

3. **The Label (y):** For each problem, we provide the correct "answer." This is our Target variable, which is 1 if the price went up in the next period and 0 if it went down or was flat.

4. **The Learning Process:** The machine learning algorithm analyzes thousands of these examples, learning the complex patterns and relationships between the features and the corresponding label. Its goal is to create an internal mathematical function, f, such that f(X) produces a result that is as close as possible to the true y.

Once this function is learned (i.e., the model is "trained"), we can give it new, unseen feature data, and it will generate a prediction about the future.

2.3 The Models of Our "Horse Race"

Our framework tests a diverse roster of supervised classification models. Each model "learns" in a different way, possessing a unique set of strengths and assumptions (an inductive bias). By testing them all, we allow the data to show us which learning style is most effective. The key models used in this book include:

- **Logistic Regression:** Despite its name, this is a core classification algorithm. It learns a simple, linear boundary between the classes. It is fast, stable, and highly interpretable, serving as an excellent baseline.

- **Decision Trees:** This model makes predictions by learning a hierarchy of simple if/then rules, creating a flowchart-like structure. While intuitive, a single decision tree is often prone to overfitting.

- **Random Forest:** A powerful ensemble method that addresses the weakness of single decision trees. It builds an entire "forest" of trees, each trained on a different random subset of the data. The final prediction is made by taking a majority vote from all the trees. This process, called **bagging**, dramatically reduces overfitting and improves robustness.

- **Gradient Boosting & XGBoost:** These are among the most powerful types of ensemble models. They also build trees, but they do so **sequentially**. Each new tree is trained specifically to correct the errors made by the previous ones. This iterative refinement allows boosting models to achieve exceptionally high performance. XGBoost (Extreme Gradient Boosting) is a highly optimized and efficient implementation of this concept.

- **Support Vector Machines (SVM):** A powerful algorithm that seeks to find the optimal boundary (or "hyperplane") that best separates the data points of the different classes with the largest possible margin. This focus on the margin often leads to excellent generalization performance.

2.4 The Critical Challenge: Overfitting

The single greatest danger in applying machine learning to noisy financial data is **overfitting**. This occurs when a model becomes too complex and, instead of learning the true, underlying market patterns (the "signal"), it begins to memorize the random fluctuations and coincidences in the training data (the "noise").

An overfit model will look like a genius on historical data, often achieving near-perfect backtest results. However, when deployed in a live market, it will fail catastrophically because the historical noise it memorized will not repeat.

Our entire four-stage pipeline is fundamentally designed as an anti-overfitting framework. Every step is a deliberate measure to combat this risk:

- **Using Simpler Models:** Our **Stage 2 "Horse Race"** allows us to compare complex models against simpler ones. If a simple LogisticRegression performs almost as well as a complex XGBoost, we have evidence that the simpler model might be more robust and less overfit.

- **Feature Selection:** Our **Stage 1 compute_feature_selection** directly reduces the risk of overfitting by decreasing the model's complexity at the source. By providing the model with a minimal set of powerful, non-redundant features, we prevent it from finding spurious patterns in irrelevant data.

- **Cross-Validation:** This is our most powerful defense. Instead of trusting a model's performance on a single dataset, we test it on multiple, different subsets of the data. This is done in **Stage 2 (Horse Race)** and **Stage 3 (Hyperparameter Tuning)**. A model that performs well consistently across all cross-validation "folds" is much more likely to have learned a generalizable signal rather than specific noise.

2.5 Evaluating Model Performance: Beyond Simple Accuracy

To guide our model selection process, we need a reliable metric of success. While **Accuracy** (the percentage of correct predictions) is intuitive, it can be dangerously misleading in trading. If a market goes up 55% of the time, a model that simply predicts "UP" every single time will have 55% accuracy but will be completely useless.

We need more nuanced metrics that measure a model's ability to balance risks and rewards.

- **Precision:** Of all the times the model predicted "BUY", how many were actually correct? *High precision helps avoid losing trades.*

- **Recall:** Of all the actual BUY opportunities that occurred, how many did the model correctly identify? *High recall helps avoid missing profitable opportunities.*

The F1-Score: The **F1-Score** is the harmonic mean of Precision and Recall. It provides a single, powerful metric that seeks a balance between these two objectives. A high F1-score indicates that the model is both reliable in its predictions (high precision) and good at finding opportunities (high recall). For this reason, our pipeline uses the **f1_weighted** score as the primary metric for judging and ranking models during the selection process.

2.6 Conclusion: Laying the Foundation

This chapter has introduced the essential machine learning concepts that form the bedrock of our trading framework. We have established that our goal is **supervised classification**, where we train models to predict market direction. We have met the roster of candidate models that will compete in our pipeline and, most importantly, we have understood that our entire process is engineered around the central challenge of **avoiding overfitting** by using robust evaluation techniques like **cross-validation** and meaningful metrics like the **F1-score**.

With this theoretical foundation in place, you are now equipped to understand the practical implementation of our four-stage pipeline in the chapters that follow.

Chapter 3: Setting Up Your Development and Trading Environment

3.1 Introduction

Before we can build sophisticated trading models, we must first construct our workshop. This chapter provides a comprehensive, step-by-step guide to setting up the complete software environment required for everything we will do in this book. We will install Python via the Anaconda distribution, which simplifies the management of the powerful data science libraries we will use. We will also install and configure the MetaTrader 5 (MT5) platform, which will be our gateway to market data and live trade execution.

Following these steps carefully will ensure you have a stable, clean, and powerful environment, providing a robust foundation for the analytical and practical work ahead. This guide is tailored for the Windows operating system.

3.2 The Core Components

Our development ecosystem consists of two primary pieces of software:

1. **The Anaconda Distribution:** This is a free, open-source distribution of Python that comes pre-packaged with essential data science libraries and tools. Crucially, it includes **Conda**, a powerful package and environment manager that allows us to create isolated workspaces for different projects, preventing conflicts between library versions.

2. **The MetaTrader 5 Terminal:** This is the trading platform provided by your broker. It will provide us with historical price data for backtesting and a live connection for executing our automated strategies.

Let's install and configure them in order.

3.3 Step 1: Installing the Anaconda Python Distribution

We will use Anaconda to manage our Python installation and libraries.

1. **Download Anaconda:**

   o Navigate to the official Anaconda download page:
     https://www.anaconda.com/download

   o Download the installer for Windows for the latest Python 3.x version.

31

2. **Install Anaconda:**

   o Run the downloaded installer executable.

   o Follow the on-screen instructions. When you reach the "Advanced Installation Options" screen, it is highly recommended that you **DO NOT** check the box that says "Add Anaconda3 to my PATH environment variable." The installer itself advises against this to avoid conflicts with other software. We will interact with Anaconda through its dedicated command prompt.

3. **Verify Installation:**

   o Once installed, open the **Anaconda Prompt** from your Windows Start Menu. It will open a command terminal.

   o In the prompt, type the following commands and press Enter after each one:

Bash

```
conda --version
python --version
```

   o If both commands return version numbers, your installation was successful.

3.4 Step 2: Installing the MetaTrader 5 Platform

Next, we install the trading platform itself.

1. **Download MetaTrader 5:**

   o Visit the official MetaTrader 5 website: https://www.metatrader5.com/

   o Click the download button and run the installer.

2. **Set Up a Trading Account:**

   o After installation, the MT5 terminal will launch.

   o Go to File -> Open an Account. Follow the prompts to either connect to your existing broker's live/demo account or open a new demo account with MetaQuotes.

   o Ensure you are logged into an account, as the Python connection requires an active session.

3.5 Step 3: Creating and Activating an Isolated Environment

To keep our project dependencies organized and avoid conflicts, we will create a dedicated virtual environment within Conda.

1. **Create a New Environment:**

    o In the **Anaconda Prompt**, run the following command to create a new environment named agnostic_trader with a specific Python version. Using a specific version ensures reproducibility.

Bash

```
conda create -n agnostic_trader python=3.9
```

    o When prompted (Proceed ([y]/n)?), type y and press Enter.

2. **Activate the Environment:**

    o Once created, you must "enter" or activate the environment each time you want to work on this project. Use the command:

Bash

```
conda activate agnostic_trader
```

    o You will know it's active because the command prompt line will now be prefixed with (agnostic_trader).

3.6 Step 4: Installing the Required Python Libraries

With our environment active, we can now install all the necessary libraries into it.

1. **Install Core Libraries with Conda:**

    o First, we install the main data science packages that are well-supported by Conda. Run the following command:

Bash

```
conda install pandas numpy scikit-learn seaborn matplotlib
```

2. **Install Specialized Libraries with Pip:**

    o For packages that are primarily distributed through the Python Package Index (PyPI), we use pip. Conda environments come with pip pre-installed. Run the following commands one by one:

33

Bash

```
pip install MetaTrader5
pip install pandas-ta
pip install xgboost
pip install imbalanced-learn
```

3. **Verify Installation (Optional):**

   o Within the active (agnostic_trader) prompt, you can type python to start the Python interpreter.

   o Then, type import pandas, import sklearn, import xgboost, import imblearn, import MetaTrader5, etc., to confirm each library can be loaded without error. Type exit() to leave the Python interpreter.

3.7 Step 5: Configuring MetaTrader 5 for Algorithmic Trading

The final configuration step is to tell the MT5 terminal that it should accept commands from our Python script.

1. In the running MT5 terminal, navigate to the menu Tools -> Options.

2. Select the **Expert Advisors** tab.

3. Check the box for **Allow algorithmic trading**.

4. It is also recommended to check the box for **Allow DLL imports** for full compatibility.

5. Click OK.

Your environment is now fully configured. Python and MetaTrader 5 are installed, and a dedicated environment contains all the tools we need to build, test, and deploy our trading models.

Chapter 4: The Principles of Strategy Validation: Backtesting and Forward Testing

4.1 Introduction: From Idea to Evidence

A trading idea, no matter how brilliant it may seem, is merely a hypothesis until it is rigorously tested. The process of transforming a speculative strategy into an evidence-based one is the cornerstone of quantitative trading. This validation process rests upon two essential pillars: **backtesting** and **forward testing**.

- **Backtesting** answers the question: "Would this strategy have worked in the past?"

- **Forward Testing** answers the question: "Is the success I saw in the past a fluke, or is it likely to generalize to a future it hasn't seen?"

This chapter will introduce the theory and practice of these vital concepts. Understanding this foundation is essential before we proceed to build our machine learning pipeline, as every stage of our framework is designed around these principles of empirical rigor.

4.2 Backtesting: Simulating Performance on Historical Data

Backtesting is the process of applying a set of trading rules to historical market data to simulate how the strategy would have performed. It is the first and most critical step in determining the potential viability of any trading idea without risking actual capital.

Why Is Backtesting Important?

1. **To Validate a Hypothesis:** Backtesting provides the first empirical "reality check" for a trading idea. A strategy that fails a backtest is unlikely to succeed in live markets and can be discarded early, saving significant time and resources.

2. **To Understand Risk and Reward:** A backtest does more than just calculate potential profit. It illuminates the strategy's risk profile, revealing crucial metrics like the maximum **drawdown** (the largest peak-to-trough loss). This allows a trader to assess if the strategy's potential volatility aligns with their personal risk tolerance.

3. **To Build Confidence:** Executing a strategy with discipline, especially during inevitable losing streaks, requires deep confidence in its long-term viability. Knowing that a strategy has successfully navigated various market conditions in the past provides the conviction needed to adhere to it in a live environment.

Key Performance Metrics in Backtesting

A thorough backtest evaluates a strategy across multiple dimensions. The most critical performance metrics include:

- **Total Return:** The overall profit or loss generated over the entire backtesting period.

- **Win Rate:** The percentage of trades that were profitable. A high win rate is desirable, but not sufficient if the average loss is much larger than the average win.

- **Maximum Drawdown:** The largest single loss from an equity peak to a subsequent trough. This is arguably the most important measure of risk.

- **Sharpe Ratio:** The primary measure of risk-adjusted return. It quantifies how much return a strategy generated for each unit of risk (volatility) it took on. A higher Sharpe Ratio is better.

- **Profit Factor:** The gross profit divided by the gross loss. A value greater than 1.0 indicates a profitable system. A value of 2.0, for example, means the strategy made \$2 for every \$1 it lost.

4.3 The Perils of Backtesting: Overfitting and Other Limitations

While indispensable, backtesting is fraught with potential pitfalls that can lead to a dangerously optimistic view of a strategy's potential.

- **Overfitting (Curve-Fitting):** This is the single greatest danger. It occurs when a strategy is fine-tuned so perfectly to historical data that it ends up fitting the random noise rather than the underlying signal. An overfit strategy looks spectacular in backtests but fails in live trading because the historical noise it memorized will not repeat.

- **Data Quality Issues:** Backtests are only as reliable as the data they are run on. Inaccurate or incomplete historical data (e.g., missing price spikes, incorrect candle data) will produce misleading results.

- **Ignoring Real-World Costs:** A simple backtest often ignores crucial real-world factors like **slippage** (the difference between the expected and actual execution price) and **transaction costs** (commissions and spreads), all of which can significantly erode profitability.

- **Non-Stationary Markets:** The past is not a perfect predictor of the future. A strategy that worked well during a five-year bull market may not be prepared for a sudden market crash or a prolonged sideways period.

It is because of these limitations, especially overfitting, that a simple backtest is not enough. We must incorporate more advanced validation techniques.

4.4 Forward Testing: Simulating the Future to Validate the Past

Forward Testing, also known as **out-of-sample testing**, is the process of testing a strategy on a period of data that was not used during the strategy's development or optimization. It is the primary tool for diagnosing overfitting.

The process is as follows:

1. Divide your historical data into two parts: an "in-sample" period (e.g., 2021-2023) and an "out-of-sample" period (e.g., 2024-2025).

2. Develop, test, and optimize your strategy using *only* the in-sample data.

3. Once you have a final, optimized strategy, you run it, without any further changes, on the out-of-sample data.

If the strategy performs well on both datasets, you have strong evidence that it has captured a genuine market edge and is not simply overfit. If it performs brilliantly on the in-sample data but poorly on the out-of-sample data, it is a classic sign of an overfit, fragile strategy that must be discarded.

4.5 How Our Pipeline Implements Validation: A Framework Clarification

It is essential to understand how these theoretical concepts are practically implemented within our specific four-stage machine learning pipeline. Our framework uses two distinct forms of testing at different stages of the process:

1. **In-Sample Validation (for Model Selection & Tuning):**

   o **What it is:** This refers to the **cross-validation** performed on the **training data** during Stage 2 (the "Model Horse Race") and Stage 3 (Hyperparameter Tuning).

   o **Its Purpose:** Its goal is to robustly *compare* candidate models and *optimize* their settings. By testing on multiple internal folds of the training data, it helps us select a champion model that is stable and performs well on data it hasn't been directly trained on, providing a strong defense against overfitting during the development phase.

2. **Out-of-Sample Validation (for Final Performance Assessment):**

   o **What it is:** This is our implementation of **forward testing**. The backtest_model function, which is called only once at the very end of the pipeline (Stage 4), is run on the **pristine test set**—the 20% of data that was held back from the very beginning and never used in any part of training, selection, or tuning.

- o **Its Purpose:** This provides the final, unbiased verdict on our champion model's ability to generalize. The performance metrics from this final backtest are our most honest estimate of how the model might perform in a live market.

4.6 Conclusion: A Foundation of Empirical Rigor

Backtesting and forward testing are not just procedural steps; they represent a philosophy of empirical rigor. They demand that every trading idea be subjected to falsification against historical evidence. By understanding these core principles—and how they are implemented through techniques like cross-validation and a held-out test set—we lay the groundwork for a development process that is disciplined and data-driven.

With this conceptual foundation in place, we are now ready to delve into the practical implementation of our advanced, machine learning-driven pipeline in the chapters to come.

Chapter 5: Building the Foundation: Extracting Historical Data with MQL5

5.1 Introduction: The Bedrock of Quantitative Research

Every quantitative trading strategy, regardless of its complexity, is built upon a single, indispensable foundation: **high-quality historical data**. This data is the bedrock upon which all subsequent analysis, feature engineering, model training, and backtesting rests. The integrity and structure of this foundational dataset directly impact the validity of every conclusion we draw and every model we build.

This chapter provides a practical guide to the very first step of our pipeline: extracting a clean, comprehensive, and analysis-ready dataset from the MetaTrader 5 (MT5) platform. We will achieve this using **MQL5**, MetaTrader's native, high-performance scripting language. The goal is to create a robust process for generating a CSV (Comma-Separated Values) file that will serve as the "single source of truth" for the entire Python-based modeling framework we will construct in the subsequent chapters.

5.2 The Tool for the Job: An Overview of MQL5

While our analysis and modeling are performed in Python, the most efficient way to access deep historical data from within the MetaTrader ecosystem is to use its native language, MQL5. MQL5 has a syntax similar to C++ and provides direct, high-speed access to the terminal's price history and trading functions. By using a simple MQL5 script, we can ensure the data is extracted accurately and formatted perfectly for our needs before we even begin our work in Python.

5.3 The Data Extraction Script: A Detailed Breakdown

The following MQL5 script is designed to be attached to any chart in MT5. It will iterate backward through the history of that chart's symbol and timeframe, writing the data for each bar into a CSV file.

The Complete MQL5 Code:

```
1. //+-----------------------------------------------------------------+
```

```mql
2.  //|                          HistoricalData|
3.  //|            Copyright 2024, MetaQuotes Software Corp. |
4.  //|                      http://www.metaquotes.net/ |
5.  //+------------------------------------------------------------------+
6.  #property strict
7.
8.  //+------------------------------------------------------------------+
9.  //| Expert initialization function                          |
10. //+------------------------------------------------------------------+
11. int OnInit()
12. {
13.    // Write headers to the CSV file
14.    WriteHeader();
15.
16.    // Get the current symbol
17.    string symbol = Symbol();
18.
19.    // Get the number of bars on the chart
20.    int bars = Bars(symbol, PERIOD_CURRENT);
21.
22.    //720 hours for each new month
23.    int from = 30720;
24.
25.
26.
27.    // Iterate over the historical bars and write the data to the CSV file
28.    Print("writing file");
29.    for (int i = 0; i <= from; i++)
30.    {
31.    MqlRates rates[];
32.    if (CopyRates(_Symbol, PERIOD_CURRENT, i, 1, rates) == 1)
33.    {
34.       string timeStr = TimeToString(rates[0].time, TIME_DATE|TIME_MINUTES);
35.       double nextClose = GetNextClose(_Symbol, rates[0].time);
36.       // WriteData function should be modified to accept a string for the time parameter
37.       WriteData(timeStr, rates[0].open, rates[0].high, rates[0].low, rates[0].close, rates[0].tick_volume,nextClose);
38.    }
39.    else
40.    {
41.       Print("Error copying historical bars at index ", i);
42.    }
43. }
44.
45.    // Return from OnInit
46.    return(INIT_SUCCEEDED);
47. }
48.
49.
50.
51.
52.
53.
54.
55. //+------------------------------------------------------------------+
56. //| Escribir encabezados en el archivo CSV                  |
57. //+------------------------------------------------------------------+
58. void WriteHeader()
59.    {
60.
61.
62.    // Create file name based on the symbol and timeframe
63.     string filename = Symbol() + "_" + string(Period()) + ".csv";
64.    string header = "Date,Open,High,Low,Close,Volume,Next_close";
65.    int file_handle=FileOpen(filename,FILE_WRITE|FILE_CSV);
66.    FileWrite(file_handle, header);
67.    FileClose(file_handle);
```

```
68.  }
69. //+------------------------------------------------------------+
70. //| Escribir datos en el archivo CSV                           |
71. //+------------------------------------------------------------+
72. void WriteData(datetime date, double open, double high, double low, double close, long volume, double nextClose)
73. {
74.    string data = TimeToString(date, TIME_DATE|TIME_MINUTES)      + "," +
75.              DoubleToString(open, _Digits)      + "," +
76.              DoubleToString(high, _Digits)      + "," +
77.              DoubleToString(low, _Digits)       + "," +
78.              DoubleToString(close, _Digits)     + "," +
79.              IntegerToString(volume)            + "," +
80.              DoubleToString(nextClose, _Digits)
81.
82.              ;
83.    // Get the timeframe as an integer
84.
85.
86.    // Create file name based on the symbol and timeframe
87.    string filename = Symbol() + "_" + string(Period()) + ".csv";
88.    // Open the file
89.    int file_handler = FileOpen(filename, FILE_READ | FILE_WRITE | FILE_CSV);
90.
91.    // Check if file is opened
92.    if(file_handler != INVALID_HANDLE)
93.    {
94.       // Move the file pointer to the end of the file
95.       FileSeek(file_handler, 0, SEEK_END);
96.
97.       // Write the data
98.       FileWrite(file_handler, data);
99.
100.      // Close the file
101.      FileClose(file_handler);
102.   }
103.   else
104.   {
105.      Print("Failed to open file: ", GetLastError());
106.   }
107. }
108. //+------------------------------------------------------------+
109. //| Obtener el próximo precio de cierre                        |
110. //+------------------------------------------------------------+
111. double GetNextClose(string symbol, datetime time)
112. {
113.    // Calculate the time of the next bar
114.    datetime nextTime = time + PeriodSeconds(PERIOD_CURRENT);
115.
116.    MqlRates rates[];
117.    if (CopyRates(symbol, PERIOD_CURRENT, nextTime, 1, rates) > 0)
118.    {
119.       return rates[0].close;
120.    }
121.    else
122.    {
123.       Print("Error al copiar el siguiente precio de cierre");
124.       return 0.0;
125.    }
126. }
127.
```

Dissecting the Code's Logic

- **The OnInit() Function:** In MQL5, scripts can have special "event handler" functions. OnInit() is one such function that is executed automatically and **only once** when the script is first loaded onto a chart. This makes it the perfect place for our one-off data export task.

- **The WriteHeader() and WriteData() Functions:** These functions handle the file operations. WriteHeader creates a new CSV file named after the symbol and timeframe (e.g., EURUSD_60.csv) and writes the header row. WriteData is designed to *append* new rows to this file by seeking to the end (SEEK_END) before writing.

- **The Data Loop:** The main loop inside OnInit iterates backward from the most recent bar (i = 0) into the past. In each iteration, CopyRates() fetches the data for a single bar.

- **The GetNextClose() Function (A Critical Design Choice):** This function's purpose is to look one step into the future *relative to the current bar being processed*. It fetches the closing price of the next bar. We do this here, during the data export, for a crucial reason: it allows us to pre-calculate the information needed for our Target variable. By including Next_close in our dataset from the start, we create a self-contained, analysis-ready file. This is far more efficient than having to calculate this relationship with pandas.shift(-1) every time we load the data in Python.

5.4 Practical Implementation: Running the Script in MetaEditor

1. **Open MetaEditor:** In your MT5 terminal, click Tools -> MetaQuotes Language Editor or press F4.

2. **Create a New Script:** In MetaEditor, click File -> New. In the wizard, select Script and give it a name (e.g., HistoricalDataExporter).

3. **Paste and Compile:** Copy the MQL5 code above and paste it into the new script file, replacing any boilerplate code. Click the Compile button (or press F7). If there are no errors, you are ready.

4. **Run on a Chart:** Return to the MT5 terminal. In the Navigator window, find your script under the Scripts section. Drag and drop it onto the chart of the instrument and timeframe you want to export (e.g., a EURUSD, H1 chart).

5. **Locate the File:** The script will run and create the CSV file. You can find it by going to File -> Open Data Folder in MT5. The file will be inside the MQL5\Files directory.

With this process complete, you now have a clean, high-fidelity historical dataset that serves as the perfect starting point for the Python-based analysis, model training, and backtesting in the chapters to come.

Chapter 6: Feature Engineering: From Raw Data to a Model-Ready Dataset

6.1 Introduction: The Art and Science of Feature Engineering

Raw price data—the open, high, low, and close—is the lifeblood of financial analysis. However, for a machine learning model, this raw data is often not in the most informative format. The process of transforming raw data into a set of structured, predictive inputs, known as **features**, is a critical discipline called **feature engineering**. This is arguably the most important step in any applied machine learning pipeline, as the quality of the features directly determines the potential performance of the final model.

This chapter provides a practical, step-by-step guide to this process. We will take the historical data CSV file extracted from MetaTrader 5 and use the power of Python and the pandas_ta library to enrich it with a diverse set of technical indicators. The output of this script is a single, clean, feature-rich dataset—the informational canvas upon which our models will learn to make predictions.

6.2 The Python Implementation: A Step-by-Step Walkthrough

The following Python script is the complete, self-contained process for preparing our data. It handles loading, cleaning, chronological ordering, feature calculation, and saving the final, analysis-ready dataset.

The Complete Data Preparation Code:

```
1. # -*- coding: utf-8 -*-
2. import os
3. import chardet
4. import pandas as pd
5. import pandas_ta as ta
6. import seaborn as sns
7. import matplotlib.pyplot as plt
8.
9. # --- Configuration ---
10. tf = "60" # Example for H1 timeframe
11. PAIR ="EURUSD"
12. filename = f"{PAIR}_{tf}.csv"
13. START_DATE = '2021-06-01'
14. END_DATE = '2025-05-16'
15.
16. print(f"Processing file: {filename} from {START_DATE} to {END_DATE}")
17.
18. # --- Data Loading and Initial Processing ---
```

```
19. with open(filename, 'rb') as f:
20.     encoding = chardet.detect(f.read())['encoding']
21. print(f"Detected encoding: {encoding}")
22.
23. df = pd.read_csv(filename, encoding=encoding)
24. # Reverse the DataFrame as MT5 exports in reverse chronological order
25. df = df.iloc[::-1].reset_index(drop=True)
26.
27. df['Date'] = pd.to_datetime(df['Date'], format='%Y.%m.%d %H:%M')
28.
29. # Filter by date range
30. df = df[(df['Date'] >= pd.to_datetime(START_DATE)) & (df['Date'] <= pd.to_datetime(END_DATE))]
31.
32. # --- Feature Engineering with Technical Indicators ---
33. print("Calculating technical indicators...")
34. df["RSI"] = ta.rsi(df["Close"], period=14)
35. df["CCI"] = ta.cci(df["High"], df["Low"], df["Close"], period=14)
36.
37. stoch = ta.stoch(df["High"], df["Low"], df["Close"], k=14, d=3)
38. if isinstance(stoch, pd.DataFrame):
39.     df["STOCHk_14_3_3"] = stoch.iloc[:, 0]
40.
41. df["ATR"] = ta.atr(df["High"], df["Low"], df["Close"], length=21)
42.
43. adx = ta.adx(df["High"], df["Low"], df["Close"], length=21)
44. if isinstance(adx, pd.DataFrame):
45.     df["ADX_21"] = adx.iloc[:, 0]
46.
47. df["Entropy"] = ta.entropy(df["Close"], length=21)
48. df["Inertia"] = ta.inertia(df["Close"], df["High"], df["Low"], length=21)
49. df["Kama"] = ta.kama(df["Close"], length=21)
50. df["VHF"] = ta.vhf(df["Close"], length=21)
51.
52. # --- Target Variable and Outlier Feature Preparation ---
53. if 'Next_close' not in df.columns:
54.     df['Next_close'] = df['Close'].shift(-1)
55.
56. df['pip_difference'] = df['Next_close'] - df['Close']
57.
58. # --- Final Cleaning and Saving ---
59. # Remove initial rows with NaN values from indicator lookback periods
60. # and the final row with a NaN value from the .shift(-1) operation.
61. df.dropna(inplace=True)
62. df.reset_index(drop=True, inplace=True)
63.
64. # Save the final dataset
65. output_filename = f"2.{PAIR}_{tf}_pandas.csv"
66. df.to_csv(output_filename, index=False)
67.
68. print(f"Processing complete. Enriched dataset saved as: {output_filename}")
69. print(f"Total rows in final dataset: {len(df)}")
70.
```

Dissecting the Code's Logic

1. **Data Loading and Preparation:** The script begins by loading the raw CSV file we created in the previous chapter. A crucial step here is df = df.iloc[::-1], which reverses the DataFrame. This corrects the reverse chronological order typical of MT5 exports, ensuring our data is properly ordered from past to present before any time-sensitive calculations are performed.

2. **Feature Engineering:** This is the core of the script. Using the pandas_ta library, we calculate a wide array of technical indicators. Each indicator is a new feature (a new column) that provides a different "lens" through which to view the market's state. We calculate momentum (RSI, CCI, Stochastic), volatility (ATR), trend strength (ADX), and more. This creates a rich "universe" of candidate features for our model selection pipeline.

3. **Preparing for the Target Variable:** The line df['Next_close'] = df['Close'].shift(-1) is a critical piece of foresight. It creates a new column where each row contains the closing price of the *next* candle. This will allow our training script to easily create the binary Target variable (e.g., Target = 1 if Next_close > Close).

4. **Data Cleaning and Finalization:** Technical indicators require a certain number of prior bars to generate their first valid value (a "lookback period"). This results in NaN (Not a Number) values at the beginning of our DataFrame. The .shift(-1) operation also creates a NaN in the very last row. The line df.dropna(inplace=True) cleanly removes all rows containing any NaN values, leaving us with a complete, pristine dataset ready for analysis. The final, enriched DataFrame is then saved to a new CSV file, clearly named to indicate it's the processed version.

6.3 The Strategic Choice: Why pandas_ta in Python?

A key architectural decision in our pipeline is to perform all feature calculations in Python using pandas_ta, rather than using the indicators built into MT5 and exporting their values. This choice is deliberate and provides several critical advantages that enhance the robustness and consistency of our entire system.

1. **Absolute Consistency:** This is the most important reason. The live trading bot will calculate features in real-time using this exact same Python library. By using pandas_ta for both historical data preparation and live feature calculation, we guarantee that the mathematical formulas and conventions are **identical**. This eliminates a subtle but potentially catastrophic source of error where a model trained on data calculated one way is asked to make predictions on live data calculated slightly differently.

2. **Unmatched Flexibility and Customization:** The pandas_ta library offers a vast collection of over 120 indicators. This provides an enormous palette for experimentation. Furthermore, within Python, we have unlimited flexibility to adjust indicator parameters or even combine multiple indicators to create novel, custom "hybrid" features—a task that would be difficult or impossible within the confines of a closed platform like MT5.

3. **Seamless Integration with the Machine Learning Pipeline:** pandas_ta is designed to work natively with pandas DataFrames, the fundamental data structure used by scikit-learn, XGBoost, and the entire Python data science ecosystem. Calculating indicators directly within our DataFrame creates a frictionless workflow, transforming the data into a feature matrix that can be fed directly into our model training pipeline without complex conversion steps.

4. **Reproducibility and Transparency:** Open-source Python code is transparent. Every step of our feature engineering process is explicitly written in this script, making it fully documented, auditable, and perfectly reproducible. This is a cornerstone of any rigorous scientific or quantitative research process.

6.4 Conclusion: Creating the Informational Canvas

With the execution of this script, we have successfully transformed raw, time-ordered price data into a rich, multi-dimensional dataset. We have created the **informational canvas** upon which our machine learning models will learn to "paint" their predictions.

This feature-engineered dataset is the final product of our data preparation phase and the primary input for the comprehensive model training and validation pipeline we will construct in the chapters ahead.

Chapter 7: Building and Evaluating Machine Learning Models with Python Based on the Agnostic Method

7.1 Model & Hyperparameter Configuration: Establishing the Experimental Universe

Before any data is processed or any model is trained, a robust machine learning pipeline must begin with a clear and deliberate definition of its experimental scope. The configuration section of our script serves this exact purpose. It acts as a centralized "control panel" where we define two critical components: the pool of candidate models for our initial evaluation and the specific "tuning knobs," or hyperparameters, we will adjust for our most promising candidates.

This separation of configuration from execution logic is a cornerstone of reproducible and maintainable research. It allows an analyst to easily modify the experimental setup without altering the core processing code.

7.1.1 The Model Roster: A Diversified Portfolio of Learners

The first part of our configuration is the MODELS list. This list defines the "horses" that will compete in our initial "horse race" to identify the most suitable modeling architecture for our specific financial dataset.

```
MODELS = [
("Logistic Regression", LogisticRegression(penalty="l2", solver="liblinear", max_iter=1000, random_state=42)),
("Random Forest", RandomForestClassifier(random_state=42)),
("Gradient Boosting", GradientBoostingClassifier(random_state=42)),
("AdaBoost", AdaBoostClassifier(random_state=42)),
("Bagging", BaggingClassifier(random_state=42)),
("XGBoost", XGBClassifier(eval_metric="logloss", use_label_encoder=False if 'use_label_encoder' in XGBClassifier().get_params()
else None, random_state=42)),
("Decision Tree", DecisionTreeClassifier(random_state=42)),
("SVM", SVC(probability=True, random_state=42)),
("K-Nearest Neighbors", KNeighborsClassifier()),
]
```

The "Why": The Importance of Diverse Inductive Biases

The choice of models is not arbitrary. It is a curated selection designed to test a wide range of **inductive biases**—the set of assumptions a model makes to generalize from finite training data. Financial markets are complex, and we do not know beforehand whether the underlying patterns are linear, non-linear, or interactive. By including models from different families, we cast a wide net:

- **Linear Models (LogisticRegression):** These models are our baseline. They assume a linear relationship between the features and the log-odds of the target outcome. They are fast, stable, and highly interpretable, but may lack the power to capture complex, non-linear market dynamics.

- **Tree-Based Models (DecisionTreeClassifier):** This model makes predictions by learning a hierarchy of simple if/then rules, effectively partitioning the feature space. It can naturally capture non-linear relationships.

- **Ensemble Models:** These are the powerhouses of modern machine learning. They combine many weak learners to create a single, strong predictor. We include two primary types:

  - **Bagging (RandomForest, BaggingClassifier):** These models work by training many decision trees on different random subsets of the data and averaging their predictions. This process, known as **Bootstrap Aggregating**, dramatically reduces variance and makes the model more stable and less prone to overfitting than a single decision tree.

  - **Boosting (GradientBoosting, AdaBoost, XGBoost):** These models build trees sequentially. Each new tree is trained to correct the errors made by the previous ones. This iterative process allows boosting models to fit complex patterns and typically achieve very high predictive performance. XGBoost is a particularly powerful and efficient implementation of this concept.

- **Instance-Based Models (KNeighborsClassifier):** This model is non-parametric, meaning it makes no assumptions about the underlying data distribution. It classifies a new data point based on the majority vote of its "k" nearest neighbors in the feature space.

- **Support Vector Machines (SVC):** This model seeks to find the optimal hyperplane that separates the two classes with the maximum possible margin, making it a powerful "maximum-margin" classifier.

By testing this diverse roster, we allow the data itself to tell us which type of model architecture is most appropriate. The structure—a list of ("Name", object) tuples—is a clean, Pythonic convention that makes it simple to iterate through and evaluate each model systematically.

7.1.2 The Hyperparameter Space: Defining the Tuning Blueprint

The second part of our configuration is the PARAM_GRIDS dictionary. This structure defines the search space for our hyperparameter tuning stage (Stage 3).

```
PARAM_GRIDS = {
```

```
    "Random Forest": {
                'classifier__n_estimators': [50, 100, 150],
                'classifier__max_depth': [5, 10, 15],
                'classifier__min_samples_leaf': [1, 5]
                },
                # ... other model grids ...
}
```

The "Why": Optimizing Model Complexity

First, it is crucial to distinguish between **parameters** and **hyperparameters**:

- **Parameters** are values learned by the model during training (e.g., the coefficients in a logistic regression).

- **Hyperparameters** are the model's external "dials" that we must set *before* training (e.g., the number of trees in a random forest).

Hyperparameter tuning is the process of finding the optimal settings for these dials. It is a critical step for balancing the **bias-variance tradeoff**. A model with too much complexity (e.g., very deep decision trees) will have low bias but high variance (overfitting). A model with too little complexity will have high bias but low variance (underfitting). Our goal is to find the "sweet spot."

The "How": The PARAM_GRIDS Structure and Syntax

The PARAM_GRIDS dictionary is structured for direct use with Scikit-learn's GridSearchCV and Pipeline objects.

- **Dictionary Keys:** The keys ("Random Forest", "XGBoost", etc.) directly match the string names we defined in our MODELS list. This allows our script to easily look up the correct tuning grid for a given model.

- **The classifier__ Syntax:** This specific syntax is essential when tuning a model inside a Pipeline. Our pipeline has named steps, such as ('scaler', StandardScaler()) and ('classifier', RandomForestClassifier()). The double underscore syntax classifier__n_estimators tells GridSearchCV, "Find the step named classifier in the pipeline, and then set its hyperparameter named n_estimators to one of the values in this list."

- **A Focused Search:** Notice that we have only defined grids for the more complex models that are likely to be top contenders and benefit most from tuning. We pragmatically choose not to define grids for every single model to conserve computational resources, focusing our efforts where they will have the greatest impact.

49

In essence, this configuration block establishes a clear, organized, and easily modifiable foundation for our entire experimental process, providing the blueprint for both the broad initial search and the focused final tuning.

7.2 Core Functions: The Building Blocks of the Pipeline

With our experimental universe defined, we now turn to the functions that execute our methodology. This section deconstructs the key Python functions responsible for data loading, feature selection, model tuning, and final backtesting. Each function serves as a modular building block in our robust development framework.

7.2.1 load_data: Data Ingestion and Sanitization

```
def load_data(filepath, hour_filter=None, minute_filter=None):    """Loads data from a CSV, filters by time, and handles outliers."""
# ... function code ...
```

The "Why": Reproducibility and Data Integrity

The journey of any model begins with data. This function serves as the sole entry point for our historical data, ensuring that the initial loading, filtering, and cleaning process is standardized and reproducible. Its responsibilities are threefold:

1. **Ingestion and Filtering:** The function loads the master dataset and immediately filters it down to the specific time slice (e.g., only hourly data from 13:00) that we are currently investigating. This allows us to build specialized models that can capture the unique market dynamics of specific trading sessions (like the London-New York overlap).

2. **Target Variable Definition:** It creates the binary Target variable by comparing the Close of the current candle with the Next_close. Target = 1 signifies an upward price movement (a "BUY" opportunity), while Target = 0 signifies a downward or flat movement (a "SELL" opportunity). This is the ground truth that our models will attempt to learn.

3. **Outlier Handling:** Financial data is often noisy, containing extreme price spikes caused by news events, liquidity gaps, or data errors. These outliers can disproportionately influence a model, causing it to learn from rare events rather than from the underlying market structure. This function implements a standard statistical method for outlier removal using the **Interquartile Range (IQR)**. It calculates the typical range of price movements (pip_difference) and removes any data points that fall far outside this range, resulting in a cleaner, more stable dataset for training.

7.2.2 compute_feature_selection: Crafting the Base Feature Set

```
1. def compute_feature_selection(X_train_data, y_train_data, ...):
2.    """Performs feature selection to find a 'Base Set'."""
3.    # ... function code ...
4.
```

The "Why": Maximizing Signal, Minimizing Noise

This function is the programmatic implementation of our **Stage 1** agnostic philosophy. Its goal is to distill a large pool of potential technical indicators into a smaller, more potent set of predictors. A model fed with too many irrelevant or redundant features can become confused, leading to slower training times and a higher risk of overfitting. This disciplined selection process is therefore critical.

7.2.3 tune_best_models: The Champion's Tune-Up

```
1. def tune_best_models(top_models_to_tune, param_grids, X_train, y_train, base_features):
2.    """Takes the best models and fine-tunes their hyperparameters with GridSearchCV."""
3.    # ... function code ...
4.
```

The "Why": Optimizing Performance Through Focused Effort

This function executes **Stage 3** of our pipeline. After the "horse race" has identified the most promising model architectures, we shift from broad exploration to focused optimization. We invest our computational budget in tuning the internal settings (hyperparameters) of these winners to unlock their maximum predictive potential for our specific problem.

The "How": Systematic Search with GridSearchCV

This function systematically iterates through the top_models_to_tune. For each one, it performs the following:

1. **Looks up the PARAM_GRIDS:** It finds the corresponding dictionary of hyperparameters to test.

2. **Initializes GridSearchCV:** This powerful Scikit-learn utility is configured to test every single combination of the specified hyperparameters.

3. **Cross-Validation:** For each combination, it performs a 3-fold stratified cross-validation, using the f1_weighted score to evaluate performance. This ensures that the chosen

hyperparameter set is one that performs well consistently across different subsets of the training data, making it more robust.

4. **Identifies the Champion:** After testing all top models, the function returns a single "champion"—the model instance with the specific combination of hyperparameters that yielded the highest average F1-score. This becomes the final model that we carry forward to the backtest.

7.2.4 backtest_model: The Final, Unbiased Examination

```
1. def backtest_model(df_test_data, model_path, features_for_model, save_folder):
2.    """Performs backtesting on the test set and generates PnL charts."""
3.    # ... function code ...
4.
```

The "Why": Assessing Generalization Performance

This function represents **Stage 4**, the final and most critical validation step. Its sole purpose is to provide an honest, unbiased evaluation of how our champion model performs on data it has never encountered during any part of the training, selection, or tuning process. The results from this function are our best available estimate of the model's potential real-world performance.

The "How": Detailed PnL Analysis

1. **Prediction on Test Set:** The function loads the saved champion model and uses it to make predictions on the df_test_data.

2. **PnL Calculation:** It calculates the Profit and Loss (PnL) for each individual trade in the test set. The calculation correctly determines profit or loss based on whether the model's prediction (Predictions) matched the actual market outcome (Target).

3. **Chronological Sorting:** Crucially, it sorts all results by Date before any cumulative calculations. This ensures the PnL curve accurately reflects the performance as it would have occurred over time.

4. **Disaggregated Reporting:** The function's key strength is its disaggregated reporting. It does not just produce one PnL curve; it produces three:

   o **Overall PnL:** The total performance, giving a top-level view.

   o **BUY Opportunities PnL:** A separate analysis of the model's performance only on instances where the market was expected to go up (Target == 1).

   o **SELL Opportunities PnL:** A separate analysis for instances where the market was expected to go down (Target == 0).

52

This detailed breakdown allows for a much deeper diagnosis of the model's behavior. It uncovers potential biases and reveals the specific market conditions under which the model excels or struggles, providing critical insights for risk management and live deployment decisions.

7.3 Main Execution Flow: Orchestrating the End-to-End Pipeline

The if __name__ == "__main__": block is the conductor of our orchestra. It is not merely a script that runs from top to bottom; it is the implementation of our entire four-stage research methodology. It systematically iterates through different market sessions, orchestrates the calls to our helper functions, and manages the flow of data from raw inputs to a final, validated, and saved model.

```
1. # --- 3. MAIN EXECUTION FLOW ---
2. if __name__ == "__main__":
3.     # Execution parameters
4.     tf = 60
5.     pair = "EURUSD"
6.     # ... other parameters
7.     N_TOP_MODELS_FOR_TUNING = 3
8.
9.     for hour in range(0, 24):
10.        for minute in range(0, 60, minute_increment):
11.            # ... function code ...
12.
```

7.3.1 The Outer Loop: Building Session-Specific Models

The "Why": The script is wrapped in a nested loop that iterates through every hour of the day (for hour in range(0, 24)). This design embodies a key hypothesis: that market behavior is not uniform throughout the day. The dynamics of the Asian session are vastly different from the London-New York overlap. By building a separate, specialized model for each distinct time segment, we aim to capture these unique session-based patterns. This is a more nuanced approach than attempting to build a single, monolithic model that must perform well under all market conditions.

The "How": For each hour and minute combination, the loop executes the entire four-stage pipeline from start to finish. It creates a dedicated folder (save_folder) for each segment, ensuring that all artifacts—the selected features, the ranked models, the final champion model, and the backtesting charts—are neatly organized and separated.

7.3.2 Data Preparation and Segregation

The "Why": This initial sub-section within the loop is dedicated to preparing a pristine and reliable dataset for the specific time segment being analyzed. It adheres to the cardinal rule of machine learning: the test data must remain completely isolated until the final evaluation.

The "How":

1. **Load and Filter:** It calls load_data() to ingest the master dataset and filter it down to the current hour and minute.

2. **Sanity Checks:** It performs critical sanity checks. If the resulting data segment is too small (len(df_full_segment) < 50) or if it contains only one class (len(y.unique()) < 2), it is impossible to build a meaningful model. In such cases, the script wisely skips to the next segment.

3. **Train-Test Split:** train_test_split is called with stratify=y. This is a crucial step that segregates 20% of the data as a "hold-out" or "test" set. The stratify argument ensures that the proportion of BUY and SELL targets in both the training and test sets mirrors the original proportion, which is vital for a fair evaluation.

4. **Resampling (SMOTETomek):** Financial datasets are often imbalanced. **SMOTE (Synthetic Minority Over-sampling Technique)** is applied *only to the training set* to correct this imbalance. It works by creating synthetic examples of the minority class, allowing the model to learn its characteristics more effectively without being overwhelmed by the majority class. This is immediately followed by Tomek Links to remove any resulting overlapping instances, cleaning up the feature space. The result is a balanced and clean training set (X_train_resampled_df, y_train_resampled) ready for modeling.

7.3.3 Staged Model Selection in Practice

The "Why": This core part of the loop is the direct implementation of our robust selection methodology. It is where the script moves methodically from a broad search to a focused conclusion.

The "How":

- **Step 1 - Base Feature Selection:** It calls compute_feature_selection() on the resampled training data to get a strong set of selected_features.

- **Step 2 - The "Horse Race":** The script iterates through the global MODELS list. For each model, it performs a 5-fold cross-validation using *only* the selected_features. It calculates the mean f1_weighted score and prints a ranked list. This provides an unbiased comparison of model architectures on a level playing field.

- **Step 3 - Fine-Tuning the Winners:** It selects the top N_TOP_MODELS_FOR_TUNING (e.g., 3) from the horse race and passes them to the tune_best_models() function. This function performs an intensive GridSearchCV to find the optimal hyperparameters for these promising candidates, ultimately returning a single, tuned champion model.

- **Step 4 - Saving and Backtesting:**

  1. The champion model—a complete Pipeline object containing the scaler and the tuned classifier—is saved to a .pkl file. The filename descriptively includes the model name, its final F1-score, the features used, and the time segment, ensuring full transparency.

  2. The backtest_model() function is called with the path to this new model and the **pristine test set** (df_test_for_backtest) that was created and isolated at the very beginning.

  3. Finally, after the backtest is complete and the final PnL is known, the script cleverly renames the saved model file to include its profit, providing an immediate, at-a-glance indicator of its out-of-sample performance.

This main execution block is the engine that drives our entire research process. It transforms the high-level philosophy of a staged, robust evaluation into a concrete, automated, and reproducible workflow, ensuring that every model produced has been subjected to the same rigorous and defensible standard of validation.

7.4 The Complete Code

```
1.
2. """
3. SCRIPT FOR TRAINING, SELECTION, AND BACKTESTING OF TRADING MODELS
4.
5. This script implements a complete Machine Learning pipeline to find
6. profitable trading models. The workflow is designed to be
7. robust and to reduce the risk of over-optimization.
8.
9. Methodology:
10. 1.  Loads and prepares a subset of data for a specific hour and minute.
11. 2.  Performs an initial feature selection to find a "Base Set".
12. 3.  Runs a "Horse Race" where all models compete using the
13.     same base feature set to identify the most promising
14.     model families.
15. 4.  Conducts a "Deep Dive" on the top 2-3 models, tuning their
16.     hyperparameters with GridSearchCV.
17. 5.  Saves the champion model (the best model after fine-tuning).
18. 6.  Performs an honest backtest on a never-before-seen test set,
19.     generating a PnL analysis for overall, buy, and sell trades.
20. """
21.
22. import os
23. import pickle
24. import datetime
25. from collections import Counter
26. from itertools import combinations
27.
28. import pandas as pd
29. import numpy as np
30. import seaborn as sns
31. import matplotlib.pyplot as plt
```

```python
32. import matplotlib.dates as mdates
33.
34. # Scikit-learn & Imblearn & XGBoost
35. from sklearn.model_selection import train_test_split, cross_val_score, StratifiedKFold, GridSearchCV
36. from sklearn.preprocessing import StandardScaler
37. from sklearn.pipeline import Pipeline
38. from imblearn.combine import SMOTETomek
39. from sklearn.feature_selection import VarianceThreshold, SelectKBest, mutual_info_classif
40. from sklearn.manifold import TSNE
41.
42. # Classifiers
43. from sklearn.linear_model import LogisticRegression, SGDClassifier
44. from sklearn.svm import SVC, NuSVC
45. from sklearn.tree import DecisionTreeClassifier
46. from sklearn.ensemble import RandomForestClassifier, GradientBoostingClassifier, AdaBoostClassifier, BaggingClassifier
47. from sklearn.neighbors import KNeighborsClassifier, RadiusNeighborsClassifier
48. from sklearn.naive_bayes import GaussianNB, BernoulliNB
49. from sklearn.discriminant_analysis import LinearDiscriminantAnalysis, QuadraticDiscriminantAnalysis
50. from xgboost import XGBClassifier
51.
52.
53. # --- 1. CONFIGURATION OF MODELS AND PARAMETERS FOR TUNING ---
54.
55. # List of models for the initial "horse race"
56. MODELS = [
57.     ("Logistic Regression", LogisticRegression(penalty="l2", solver="liblinear", max_iter=1000, random_state=42)),
58.     ("Random Forest", RandomForestClassifier(random_state=42)),
59.     ("Gradient Boosting", GradientBoostingClassifier(random_state=42)),
60.     ("AdaBoost", AdaBoostClassifier(random_state=42)),
61.     ("Bagging", BaggingClassifier(random_state=42)),
62.     ("XGBoost", XGBClassifier(eval_metric="logloss", use_label_encoder=False if 'use_label_encoder' in
XGBClassifier().get_params() else None, random_state=42)),
63.     ("Decision Tree", DecisionTreeClassifier(random_state=42)),
64.     ("SVM", SVC(probability=True, random_state=42)),
65.     ("K-Nearest Neighbors", KNeighborsClassifier()),
66. ]
67.
68. # Parameter grid for fine-tuning the best models (GridSearchCV)
69. PARAM_GRIDS = {
70.     "Random Forest": {
71.         'classifier__n_estimators': [50, 100, 150],
72.         'classifier__max_depth': [5, 10, 15],
73.         'classifier__min_samples_leaf': [1, 5]
74.     },
75.     "Gradient Boosting": {
76.         'classifier__n_estimators': [50, 100, 150],
77.         'classifier__learning_rate': [0.01, 0.05, 0.1],
78.         'classifier__max_depth': [3, 5, 7]
79.     },
80.     "XGBoost": {
81.         'classifier__n_estimators': [50, 100, 150],
82.         'classifier__learning_rate': [0.01, 0.05, 0.1],
83.         'classifier__max_depth': [3, 5, 7]
84.     },
85.     "Logistic Regression": {
86.         'classifier__C': [0.1, 1.0, 10.0]
87.     },
88.     "AdaBoost": {
89.         'classifier__n_estimators': [50, 100, 200],
90.         'classifier__learning_rate': [0.01, 0.1, 1.0]
91.     },
92.     "SVM": {
93.         'classifier__C': [0.1, 1, 10],
94.         'classifier__gamma': ['scale', 'auto']
95.     }
96. }
```

```
97.
98.
99. # --- 2. FUNCTION DEFINITIONS ---
100.
101. def load_data(filepath, hour_filter=None, minute_filter=None):
102.     """Loads data from a CSV, filters by time, and handles outliers."""
103.     try:
104.         df = pd.read_csv(filepath, parse_dates=['Date'])
105.     except FileNotFoundError:
106.         print(f"Error: Data file not found at {filepath}")
107.         return pd.DataFrame()
108.
109.     if hour_filter is not None:
110.         df = df[df['Date'].dt.hour == hour_filter]
111.     if minute_filter is not None:
112.         df = df[df['Date'].dt.minute == minute_filter]
113.
114.     if df.empty:
115.         print(f"No data after filtering for hour {hour_filter}, minute {minute_filter}.")
116.         return df
117.
118.     if 'Next_close' in df.columns and 'Close' in df.columns:
119.         df['Target'] = (df['Next_close'] > df['Close']).astype(int)
120.     else:
121.         print("Warning: Could not create 'Target' column.")
122.         return pd.DataFrame()
123.
124.     if 'pip_difference' in df.columns:
125.         Q1, Q3 = df['pip_difference'].quantile(0.25), df['pip_difference'].quantile(0.75)
126.         IQR = Q3 - Q1
127.         lower_bound, upper_bound = Q1 - 1.5 * IQR, Q3 + 1.5 * IQR
128.
129.         rows_before = len(df)
130.         df = df[(df['pip_difference'] >= lower_bound) & (df['pip_difference'] <= upper_bound)]
131.         print(f"Outliers removed by 'pip_difference': {rows_before - len(df)}")
132.
133.     return df
134.
135. def compute_feature_selection(X_train_data, y_train_data, initial_feature_pool, correlation_threshold=0.7,
     variance_threshold=0.01, k_best=5):
136.     """Performs feature selection to find a 'Base Set'."""
137.     print(f"\n--- STEP 1: Base Feature Selection ---")
138.     print(f"Initial feature pool: {initial_feature_pool}")
139.
140.     if X_train_data.empty: return []
141.
142.     X_train_pool = X_train_data[initial_feature_pool].copy()
143.
144.     # 1. Low Variance
145.     selector_var = VarianceThreshold(threshold=variance_threshold)
146.     selector_var.fit(X_train_pool)
147.     features_var = X_train_pool.columns[selector_var.get_support()]
148.     print(f"Features after variance filter: {list(features_var)}")
149.     if len(features_var) == 0: return []
150.
151.     # 2. Mutual Information (K-Best)
152.     k = min(k_best, len(features_var))
153.     selector_kbest = SelectKBest(score_func=mutual_info_classif, k=k)
154.     selector_kbest.fit(X_train_pool[features_var], y_train_data)
155.     features_kbest = features_var[selector_kbest.get_support()]
156.     print(f"Top {k} features by Mutual Information: {list(features_kbest)}")
157.     if len(features_kbest) == 0: return []
158.
159.     # 3. Correlation
160.     corr_matrix = X_train_pool[features_kbest].corr().abs()
161.     upper_tri = corr_matrix.where(np.triu(np.ones(corr_matrix.shape), k=1).astype(bool))
```

57

```python
162.    to_drop = [column for column in upper_tri.columns if any(upper_tri[column] > correlation_threshold)]
163.    print(f"Features removed due to high correlation (> {correlation_threshold}): {to_drop}")
164.
165.    final_features = [f for f in features_kbest if f not in to_drop]
166.    print(f"Final Base Feature Set: {final_features}")
167.
168.    return final_features
169.
170. def tune_best_models(top_models_to_tune, param_grids, X_train, y_train, base_features):
171.     """Takes the best models and fine-tunes their hyperparameters with GridSearchCV."""
172.     print("\n--- STEP 3: Deep Dive & Hyperparameter Tuning ---")
173.
174.     best_overall_model = None
175.     best_overall_score = -1
176.     X_train_subset = X_train[base_features]
177.
178.     for model_name, model_instance in top_models_to_tune:
179.         if model_name not in param_grids:
180.             print(f"No parameter grid defined for '{model_name}'. Skipping tuning.")
181.             continue
182.
183.         print(f"Tuning hyperparameters for: {model_name}...")
184.         pipeline = Pipeline([('scaler', StandardScaler()), ('classifier', model_instance)])
185.
186.         grid_search = GridSearchCV(
187.             estimator=pipeline, param_grid=param_grids[model_name], scoring='f1_weighted',
188.             cv=StratifiedKFold(n_splits=3, shuffle=True, random_state=42), n_jobs=-1, verbose=0
189.         )
190.         grid_search.fit(X_train_subset, y_train)
191.
192.         print(f"Best F1-Weighted score for {model_name}: {grid_search.best_score_:.4f}")
193.         print(f"Best parameters: {grid_search.best_params_}")
194.
195.         if grid_search.best_score_ > best_overall_score:
196.             best_overall_score = grid_search.best_score_
197.             best_overall_model = {
198.                 "name": model_name, "score": grid_search.best_score_,
199.                 "pipeline": grid_search.best_estimator_, "features": base_features
200.             }
201.
202.     if best_overall_model:
203.         print("-" * 50)
204.         print(f"🏆 Champion Model from Tuning: {best_overall_model['name']} with F1-Score of {best_overall_model['score']:.4f}")
205.     else:
206.         print("Could not determine a champion model from tuning.")
207.
208.     return best_overall_model
209.
210. def backtest_model(df_test_data, model_path, features_for_model, save_folder):
211.     """Performs backtesting on the test set and generates PnL charts."""
212.     if df_test_data.empty:
213.         print("No test data provided for backtesting.")
214.         return 0.0
215.
216.     if not features_for_model:
217.         print("No features provided for backtesting.")
218.         return 0.0
219.
220.     X_test_predict_subset = df_test_data[list(features_for_model)].copy()
221.
222.     try:
223.         with open(model_path, 'rb') as f:
224.             pipeline_loaded = pickle.load(f)
225.     except Exception as e:
226.         print(f"Error loading model {model_path}: {e}")
227.         return 0.0
```

```
228.
229.    if X_test_predict_subset.isnull().values.any():
230.        print("Warning: NaNs found in test data. Filling with mean.")
231.        X_test_predict_subset = X_test_predict_subset.fillna(X_test_predict_subset.mean())
232.
233.    df_backtest_results = df_test_data.copy()
234.    df_backtest_results['Predictions'] = pipeline_loaded.predict(X_test_predict_subset)
235.    df_backtest_results['Target'] = df_backtest_results['Target'].astype(int)
236.    df_backtest_results['PnL'] = 0.0
237.
238.    for index, row in df_backtest_results.iterrows():
239.        pnl_val = 0.0
240.        pip_value_multiplier = 10000 * 10
241.        if row['Target'] == 0: # SELL opportunity
242.            pnl_val = (row['Close'] - row['Next_close']) if row['Predictions'] == 0 else (row['Next_close'] - row['Close'])
243.        else: # BUY opportunity
244.            pnl_val = (row['Next_close'] - row['Close']) if row['Predictions'] == 1 else (row['Close'] - row['Next_close'])
245.        df_backtest_results.loc[index, 'PnL'] = round(pnl_val * pip_value_multiplier, 4)
246.
247.    df_backtest_results = df_backtest_results.sort_values(by='Date')
248.    df_backtest_results['Correct_Prediction'] = (df_backtest_results['Predictions'] == df_backtest_results['Target'])
249.
250.    print(f"\n--- Backtesting Results ---")
251.
252.    # --- 1. Overall PnL and Chart ---
253.    df_backtest_results['Cumulative PnL (Overall)'] = round(df_backtest_results['PnL'].cumsum(), 4)
254.    final_pnl_overall = df_backtest_results['Cumulative PnL (Overall)'].iloc[-1] if not df_backtest_results.empty else 0
255.    print(f"Total trades in Test Set: {len(df_backtest_results)}")
256.    print(f"Final PnL (Overall): {final_pnl_overall:.2f} USD")
257.
258.    if not df_backtest_results.empty:
259.        plt.figure(figsize=(12, 6))
260.        plt.plot(df_backtest_results['Date'], df_backtest_results['Cumulative PnL (Overall)'], label='Cumulative PnL (All Trades)',
color='purple')
261.        plt.xlabel('Date'); plt.ylabel('Profit & Loss ($)')
262.        plt.title(f'Overall Backtesting Performance - Model: {os.path.basename(model_path)}')
263.        plt.legend(); plt.gca().xaxis.set_major_formatter(mdates.DateFormatter('%Y-%m-%d')); plt.gcf().autofmt_xdate()
264.        plot_filename_overall = os.path.basename(model_path).replace(".pkl", f"_profitOverall{final_pnl_overall:.2f}_plot.png")
265.        plt.savefig(os.path.join(save_folder, plot_filename_overall)); plt.close()
266.        print(f"Overall backtest plot saved to: {plot_filename_overall}")
267.
268.    # --- 2. PnL and Chart for BUY Opportunities (Target == 1) ---
269.    df_buy_ops = df_backtest_results[df_backtest_results['Target'] == 1].copy()
270.    print(f"Found {len(df_buy_ops)} BUY opportunities in the test set.")
271.
272.    final_pnl_buy = 0.0
273.    if not df_buy_ops.empty:
274.        df_buy_ops['Cumulative PnL (BUY)'] = round(df_buy_ops['PnL'].cumsum(), 4)
275.        final_pnl_buy = df_buy_ops['Cumulative PnL (BUY)'].iloc[-1]
276.
277.        plt.figure(figsize=(12, 6))
278.        plt.plot(df_buy_ops['Date'], df_buy_ops['Cumulative PnL (BUY)'], label='Cumulative PnL (BUY Opportunities)',
color='green')
279.        plt.xlabel('Date'); plt.ylabel('Profit & Loss ($)')
280.        plt.title(f'Backtesting for BUY Opportunities - Model: {os.path.basename(model_path)}')
281.        plt.legend(); plt.gca().xaxis.set_major_formatter(mdates.DateFormatter('%Y-%m-%d')); plt.gcf().autofmt_xdate()
282.        plot_filename_buy = os.path.basename(model_path).replace(".pkl", f"_profitBUY{final_pnl_buy:.2f}_plot.png")
283.        plt.savefig(os.path.join(save_folder, plot_filename_buy)); plt.close()
284.        print(f"BUY opportunities backtest plot saved to: {plot_filename_buy}")
285.
286.    print(f"Final PnL (BUY Opportunities): {final_pnl_buy:.2f} USD")
287.
288.    # --- 3. PnL and Chart for SELL Opportunities (Target == 0) ---
289.    df_sell_ops = df_backtest_results[df_backtest_results['Target'] == 0].copy()
290.    print(f"Found {len(df_sell_ops)} SELL opportunities in the test set.")
291.
```

```
292.    final_pnl_sell = 0.0
293.    if not df_sell_ops.empty:
294.        df_sell_ops['Cumulative PnL (SELL)'] = round(df_sell_ops['PnL'].cumsum(), 4)
295.        final_pnl_sell = df_sell_ops['Cumulative PnL (SELL)'].iloc[-1]
296.
297.        plt.figure(figsize=(12, 6))
298.        plt.plot(df_sell_ops['Date'], df_sell_ops['Cumulative PnL (SELL)'], label='Cumulative PnL (SELL Opportunities)', color='red')
299.        plt.xlabel('Date'); plt.ylabel('Profit & Loss ($)')
300.        plt.title(f'Backtesting for SELL Opportunities - Model: {os.path.basename(model_path)}')
301.        plt.legend(); plt.gca().xaxis.set_major_formatter(mdates.DateFormatter('%Y-%m-%d')); plt.gcf().autofmt_xdate()
302.        plot_filename_sell = os.path.basename(model_path).replace(".pkl", f"_profitSELL{final_pnl_sell:.2f}_plot.png")
303.        plt.savefig(os.path.join(save_folder, plot_filename_sell)); plt.close()
304.        print(f"SELL opportunities backtest plot saved to: {plot_filename_sell}")
305.
306.    print(f"Final PnL (SELL Opportunities): {final_pnl_sell:.2f} USD")
307.
308.    # ... (code to save the CSV can be added here) ...
309.
310.    return final_pnl_overall
311.
312. # --- 3. MAIN EXECUTION FLOW ---
313. if __name__ == "__main__":
314.     # Execution parameters
315.     tf = 60
316.     pair = "EURUSD"
317.     start_date_label, end_date_label = "20230101", "20250515"
318.     minute_increment = tf
319.     N_TOP_MODELS_FOR_TUNING = 3 # Number of models to pass to the fine-tuning stage
320.
321.     for hour in range(0, 24):
322.         for minute in range(0, 60, minute_increment):
323.             print(f"\n{'='*20} PROCESSING: Hour={hour}, Minute={minute} {'='*20}")
324.
325.             # --- DATA PREPARATION ---
326.             save_folder = f"{pair}_hour{hour}_minute{minute}_model_results"
327.             os.makedirs(save_folder, exist_ok=True)
328.             filepath = f"2.{pair}_{tf}_pandas.csv"
329.
330.             df_full_segment = load_data(filepath, hour_filter=hour, minute_filter=minute)
331.
332.             if df_full_segment.empty or 'Target' not in df_full_segment.columns or len(df_full_segment) < 50:
333.                 print("Insufficient data for this segment. Skipping.")
334.                 continue
335.
336.             all_potential_features = ["CCI", 'ATR', 'STOCHk_14_3_3', 'ADX_21', 'Entropy', "Inertia", "Kama", "VHF", "RSI"]
337.             X_features_available = [f for f in all_potential_features if f in df_full_segment.columns]
338.
339.             X = df_full_segment[X_features_available]
340.             y = df_full_segment['Target']
341.
342.             if len(y.unique()) < 2:
343.                 print(f"Not enough classes in Target (found: {len(y.unique())}). Skipping.")
344.                 continue
345.
346.             X_train, X_test, y_train, y_test = train_test_split(X, y, test_size=0.2, random_state=42, stratify=y)
347.
348.             # Fill NaNs and apply SMOTE
349.             X_train.fillna(X_train.mean(), inplace=True)
350.             smote_tomek = SMOTETomek(random_state=42)
351.             try:
352.                 X_train_resampled, y_train_resampled = smote_tomek.fit_resample(X_train, y_train)
353.                 X_train_resampled_df = pd.DataFrame(X_train_resampled, columns=X_train.columns)
354.             except Exception as e:
355.                 print(f"Error during SMOTE (possibly too few samples in one class): {e}. Skipping.")
356.                 continue
357.
```

```python
358.    # --- STEP 1: Base Feature Selection ---
359.    selected_features = compute_feature_selection(
360.        X_train_resampled_df, y_train_resampled,
361.        initial_feature_pool=X_features_available, k_best=7
362.    )
363.    if not selected_features:
364.        print("No features were selected. Skipping to the next segment.")
365.        continue
366.
367.    # --- STEP 2: Model "Horse Race" ---
368.    print("\n--- STEP 2: Model 'Horse Race' ---")
369.
370.    horse_race_results = []
371.    for name, model_instance in MODELS:
372.        pipeline = Pipeline([('scaler', StandardScaler()), ('classifier', model_instance)])
373.        try:
374.            scores = cross_val_score(pipeline, X_train_resampled_df[selected_features], y_train_resampled,
375.                        cv=StratifiedKFold(n_splits=5, shuffle=True, random_state=42),
376.                        scoring='f1_weighted')
377.            horse_race_results.append({"name": name, "score": scores.mean()})
378.        except Exception as e:
379.            print(f'Error evaluating {name}: {e}")
380.
381.    if not horse_race_results:
382.        print("No models could be evaluated. Skipping.")
383.        continue
384.
385.    horse_race_results.sort(key=lambda x: x['score'], reverse=True)
386.    print("\n--- Model Ranking (Horse Race) ---")
387.    for res in horse_race_results: print(f'Model: {res['name']:<25} | Score: {res['score']:.4f}")
388.
389.    # --- STEP 3: Fine-Tuning of Best Models ---
390.    top_model_names = [res['name'] for res in horse_race_results[:N_TOP_MODELS_FOR_TUNING]]
391.    top_models_to_tune = [m for m in MODELS if m[0] in top_model_names]
392.
393.    best_tuned_result = tune_best_models(
394.        top_models_to_tune, PARAM_GRIDS, X_train_resampled_df, y_train_resampled, selected_features
395.    )
396.    if not best_tuned_result:
397.        print("The tuning process did not find a winning model. Skipping.")
398.        continue
399.
400.    # --- STEP 4: Saving and Backtesting the Champion Model ---
401.    print("\n--- STEP 4: Saving and Backtesting the Champion Model ---")
402.
403.    champion_pipeline = best_tuned_result['pipeline']
404.    champion_features = best_tuned_result['features']
405.
406.    filename = (f"{pair}_{best_tuned_result['name'].replace(' ', '')}_f1w_{best_tuned_result['score']:.4f}_TUNED_"
407.               f"features_{'_'.join(champion_features)}_tf{tf}_hour{hour}_minute{minute}.pkl")
408.    model_filepath = os.path.join(save_folder, filename)
409.
410.    with open(model_filepath, "wb") as f:
411.        pickle.dump(champion_pipeline, f)
412.    print(f'Champion model saved as: {model_filepath}")
413.
414.    df_test_for_backtest = df_full_segment.loc[X_test.index].copy()
415.    final_pnl = backtest_model(
416.        df_test_for_backtest, model_filepath, champion_features, save_folder
417.    )
418.
419.    if os.path.exists(model_filepath):
420.        new_basename = f'profit_{final_pnl:.2f}_{os.path.basename(model_filepath)}"
421.        new_filepath = os.path.join(save_folder, new_basename)
422.        try:
423.            os.rename(model_filepath, new_filepath)
```

```
424.            print(f"Model file renamed to: {new_filepath}")
425.        except Exception as e:
426.            print(f"Error renaming model file: {e}")
427.
428.        print(f"--- Processing complete for hour={hour}, minute={minute} ---")
429.
430.    print("\nProcessing of all segments finished.")
431.
```

Chapter 8: A Principled Framework for Feature and Model Selection

8.1 The Allure and Peril of Exhaustive Search

In the quest to build the most predictive machine learning model, a tempting but treacherous path is that of the exhaustive or "inverse" search. This approach, born from the desire to leave no stone unturned, posits that by testing every conceivable combination of features, one can empirically discover the single optimal subset that unlocks the data's hidden patterns. It is a philosophy of pure, data-driven agnosticism: make no assumptions, test everything, and let the highest score win.

While theoretically comprehensive, this methodology falls into a well-known statistical trap: the **curse of dimensionality** and the **multiple testing problem**. When a vast number of experiments are conducted, the probability of finding a seemingly significant result by sheer random chance approaches 100%. The model that emerges from such a search is often not a robust predictor but a fragile, over-optimized fluke—a "winner" cursed to fail when faced with new, unseen data.

Recognizing this peril, the pipeline implemented in our code deliberately rejects the brute-force strategy. Instead, it adopts a **principled, four-stage funneling methodology**. This framework is designed to systematically reduce complexity and focus computational effort, ensuring that our final model is not the luckiest, but the most robust.

8.2 The Building Blocks: Understanding Classical Feature Selection

To appreciate our methodology, it is helpful to understand the classical approaches it builds upon. These methods are typically categorized as follows:

- **Filter Methods:** These techniques apply statistical measures to score features based on their individual relevance to the target variable, *before* any modeling is done. Examples include correlation coefficients and **Mutual Information**, which our pipeline uses in its first stage to identify relevant features.

- **Wrapper Methods:** This approach uses a specific machine learning model to evaluate the utility of different feature subsets. The exhaustive search described in the original chapter text is a type of wrapper method. A more guided example is Recursive Feature Elimination (RFE), where a model recursively removes the least important feature until an optimal set is found.

- **Embedded Methods:** Some algorithms have built-in mechanisms for feature selection. Models using L1 (Lasso) regularization, for instance, can shrink the coefficients of less important features to zero, effectively selecting a simpler feature set. Tree-based models like Random Forest and XGBoost inherently perform feature selection by choosing the most informative features at each split.

Our pipeline strategically combines the strengths of these approaches: it uses a sophisticated **filter** method to create a strong initial candidate pool, then uses model performance (akin to a **wrapper** method) to identify the best model architectures, many of which have powerful **embedded** selection capabilities.

8.3 The Implemented Pipeline: From Broad Exploration to Focused Tuning

The core of our script is the implementation of a structured, four-stage workflow. Let's examine how the code executes this strategy.

8.3.1 Stage 1: Foundational Feature Selection

Instead of beginning a combinatorial search, our first step (compute_feature_selection function) is to craft a single, high-quality **Base Feature Set**. We do not test combinations here; we filter our initial pool of all available indicators to find a subset that is both relevant and non-redundant. This is a crucial first step in noise reduction and is fundamental to building a stable model.

8.3.2 Stage 2: The Model "Horse Race"

With our Base Feature Set in hand, we seek to answer a critical question: *What type of model architecture is best suited for this data?* We do this by making all models compete on a level playing field. The script iterates through the MODELS list, and using cross_val_score, evaluates each one on the exact same set of features. This tells us if the underlying patterns are better captured by linear models, tree-based ensembles, or other types of learners. This is a far more insightful and efficient exploration than blindly testing feature subsets.

8.3.3 Stage 3: Hyperparameter Tuning

Only after identifying the top 2-3 winning architectures from the horse race do we proceed to the computationally expensive step of tuning. The tune_best_models function uses GridSearchCV to optimize the internal "dials" (hyperparameters) of these promising candidates. This ensures we are focusing our resources on models that have already proven their suitability for the problem, sharpening our best tools rather than wasting time on those that are fundamentally a poor fit.

8.4 Why This Structured Approach is Superior to an "Inverse" Search

The original chapter text extolled the virtues of an exhaustive search, but it's vital to understand the trade-offs and why our structured approach is superior for a domain as noisy as financial markets.

1. Mitigation of Overfitting and the "Winner's Curse"

The primary flaw of an exhaustive "inverse" search is the exponential growth of the search space. For a set of n features, there are 2n possible subsets.

$$Total\ Subsets\ = \sum_{k=0}^{n} \binom{n}{k} = 2^n$$

- For 10 features, this is $2^{10} = 1,024$ combinations.

- For just 20 features, this is $2^{20} = 1,048,576$ combinations.

Testing over a million model configurations makes it statistically inevitable that one will perfectly align with the noise in the training data. Our funnel-based approach drastically reduces the number of "experiments," thereby minimizing the risk of capitalizing on spurious correlations.

2. Discovering True Synergies vs. Random Interactions

While an exhaustive search *can* uncover feature synergies, it has no way of distinguishing between a genuine, robust interaction and a random one specific to the training set.

Our approach uncovers synergies more intelligently. Strong models like XGBoost and RandomForest are specifically designed to model complex, non-linear interactions *internally*. By feeding them a well-curated, non-redundant set of features (from Stage 1), we empower the algorithm to find the meaningful interactions itself, a process that is far more robust than randomly stumbling upon a "magic" combination.

3. Computational Feasibility

The exponential growth of the exhaustive search makes it computationally infeasible for any non-trivial number of features. Our structured approach, while still intensive during the GridSearchCV stage, is practical. It focuses expensive computation only on a few promising candidates, making the entire workflow achievable.

4. Insight over a "Black Box" Answer

The brute-force method outputs a single "best" combination with little context. Our methodology provides valuable insights at each stage:

- **Stage 1:** Tells us which individual features are most relevant.

- **Stage 2:** Tells us which *family* of models is most effective.

- **Stage 3:** Tells us the optimal configuration for those models.

This builds a deep understanding of the problem, which is far more valuable than a single, potentially random "answer."

8.5 Conclusion: From Exhaustive Search to Intelligent Exploration

The allure of testing every possibility is strong, but it is a siren's call that often leads to overfit and unreliable models. The methodology implemented in our code represents a paradigm shift from a naïve, exhaustive search to a mature, **intelligent exploration**. It acknowledges the complexity of financial markets and embeds principles of statistical robustness at every step. By systematically filtering, ranking, and tuning, we build a compelling case for our final model, ensuring it is chosen not because it was the luckiest in a lottery of combinations, but because it demonstrated superior, stable, and validated performance through a rigorous and defensible process.

Chapter 9: The Parsimony Principle in Financial Modeling: The Surprising Efficacy of Minimal Feature Sets

9.1 The Paradox of Complexity in Financial Forecasting

In the quantitative analysis of financial markets—a domain characterized by its immense complexity and high dimensionality—a powerful paradox emerges. Intuition suggests that to model such a multifaceted system, one must employ an equally complex apparatus. The temptation is to construct models that incorporate a vast array of features, from dozens of technical indicators to fundamental economic data and alternative sentiment metrics, under the assumption that more information must invariably lead to superior predictive power.

However, empirical evidence and foundational principles of statistical learning often reveal a counterintuitive truth: models of disciplined simplicity frequently outperform their more complex counterparts. This phenomenon, where minimal feature sets yield more robust and reliable results, is not an anomaly but rather a direct consequence of the inherent nature of financial data and the mathematical principles that govern model generalization.

This chapter provides a deep dive into this paradox. We will explore the statistical reasoning—including the principle of parsimony, the bias-variance tradeoff, and the curse of dimensionality—that explains why "less is often more" in feature selection. Crucially, we will demonstrate how the structured, multi-stage pipeline developed in this book is not merely a matter of convenience, but a deliberate and necessary framework designed to enforce this principle and build models that thrive in the unforgiving environment of live markets.

9.2 The Theoretical Foundations for a Minimalist Approach

The preference for simpler models is not an arbitrary aesthetic choice; it is grounded in decades of statistical theory and practical application.

a. The Principle of Parsimony and the Bias-Variance Tradeoff

At the heart of our methodology lies **Occam's Razor**, the philosophical principle which posits that "entities should not be multiplied without necessity." In machine learning, this is known as the **Principle of Parsimony**. It dictates that, given competing models with similar explanatory power, the simplest one—the one with the fewest assumptions and fewest features—should be preferred.

This principle is the practical manifestation of one of the most fundamental concepts in machine learning: the **bias-variance tradeoff**.

- **Bias** is the error introduced by approximating a complex, real-world problem with a simpler model. A model with high bias pays little attention to the training data and oversimplifies, leading to underfitting.

- **Variance** is the error from a model's excessive sensitivity to the small fluctuations in the training data. A model with high variance pays *too much* attention to the training data, fitting the noise rather than the signal. This leads to **overfitting**.

Adding more features to a model almost always decreases its bias (as it can fit the training data more closely) but at the cost of increasing its variance. The goal of a robust modeling process is to find the "sweet spot" that minimizes the total error. In the noisy domain of finance, the risk of high variance (overfitting) is exceptionally high. A complex model can easily find phantom patterns in historical noise, leading to a spectacular backtest but disastrous live performance.

How Our Pipeline Enforces Parsimony: Our framework actively manages this tradeoff from the very beginning. **Stage 1 (compute_feature_selection)** is a dedicated engine for enforcing parsimony. It systematically attacks model complexity at its source: the features. By filtering for variance, selecting for relevance via Mutual Information, and pruning for redundancy via correlation analysis, it constructs a minimal, high-signal feature set. This act of starting with a simple, potent set of inputs is a deliberate strategy to control model variance before a single model is even trained.

b. The Curse of Dimensionality and Model Overfitting

As we add more features (dimensions) to our dataset, the volume of the feature space grows exponentially. This leads to a phenomenon known as the **Curse of Dimensionality**. As the space expands, the available data points become increasingly sparse, making it much harder to establish statistically significant relationships. From a geometric perspective, the distance between any two points in a high-dimensional space becomes vast and less meaningful.

A model operating in this sparse, high-dimensional space can be easily misled. It can find "pockets" of noise that appear to be predictive patterns simply because there are no nearby counterexamples in the training data. This is a primary driver of overfitting.

Our Structured Approach as the Antidote: The brute-force "inverse selection" strategy, which tests an exponential number of feature combinations, is a direct invitation to the Curse of Dimensionality. It actively explores the sparsest, most dangerous regions of the feature space in search of a "lucky" combination.

Our pipeline acts as a direct countermeasure.

1. By aggressively reducing the number of features in **Stage 1**, we fundamentally lower the dimensionality of the problem.

2. By conducting the **"Horse Race" (Stage 2)** on a fixed, low-dimensional feature set, we prevent the models from exploring these perilous high-dimensional combinations.

3. By focusing on **Hyperparameter Tuning (Stage 3)**, we optimize the model's behavior *within* this safer, lower-dimensional space.

c. Feature Synergies and the Trap of Multicollinearity

Financial markets are replete with interactive effects. The predictive power of a volatility indicator, for instance, may depend on the prevailing trend. While it is crucial to capture these **synergies**, the brute-force search for them is inefficient and risky.

A more significant and insidious problem is **multicollinearity**, where features are highly correlated with one another. Including multiple redundant features (e.g., three different short-term momentum oscillators) provides no new information to the model. Instead, it can destabilize the model's learned parameters, reduce the interpretability of feature importance, and mask the true drivers of its predictions.

Discovering Synergies Intelligently: Our pipeline addresses both issues intelligently.

- The correlation filter in **Stage 1** directly removes redundant features, tackling multicollinearity at the source.

- True synergies are best discovered not by random chance, but by powerful algorithms designed for the task. In **Stage 2**, when we identify models like XGBoost or RandomForest as top performers, we are selecting architectures that are inherently capable of modeling complex, non-linear interactions *internally*. By feeding these powerful models a clean, non-redundant set of inputs, we empower them to find the genuine synergies, a far more robust approach than hoping to stumble upon them in a combinatorial lottery.

9.3 The Practical Advantages of a Minimalist Framework

Adopting this disciplined, parsimonious approach yields tangible benefits that extend beyond statistical theory.

a. Enhanced Interpretability, Trust, and Accountability

In any high-stakes field, a "black box" model is a liability. A model that relies on 47 different inputs is virtually impossible to interpret. If it succeeds, we don't know why. If it fails, we don't know how to fix it. This lack of transparency makes it impossible for stakeholders, risk managers, or even the quant who built it to trust its decisions.

A model derived from our pipeline, however, is highly interpretable. If the champion model uses only ['ADX_21', 'ATR', 'Inertia'], we can articulate its logic precisely: "This model makes decisions based on trend strength, volatility, and momentum persistence." This transparency fosters trust, facilitates debugging, and creates a clear line of accountability for the model's behavior.

b. Computational Efficiency and Research Velocity

The computational argument is stark. As noted previously, the number of feature subsets grows exponentially (2n). In contrast, our structured pipeline's complexity grows linearly with the number of models in the "horse race" and polynomially during the constrained GridSearchCV step.

This is not just a matter of saving electricity. It dramatically accelerates the **research and development cycle**. The ability to rapidly iterate, test new hypotheses, and re-validate models for different time windows is a significant competitive advantage. A process that takes hours instead of weeks allows for more robust and timely model development.

c. Superior Robustness to Market Regime Shifts

Financial markets are non-stationary; they cycle through different **regimes** (e.g., high-volatility trending, low-volatility range-bound). A complex model with many features is highly susceptible to being overfit to the specific regime present in its training data. When the market inevitably shifts, the model's performance collapses.

A simpler model, built upon a minimal set of features representing fundamental market principles (like trend, momentum, volatility), is inherently more robust. Because it has not learned the intricate, specific noise of a single regime, it is more likely to remain effective when the market's character changes. Its simplicity grants it flexibility and resilience, which are paramount for long-term survival in dynamic markets.

9.4 Conclusion: The Discipline of Simplicity

The surprising effectiveness of minimal feature sets is not an argument against comprehensive data analysis. Rather, it is an argument for a **disciplined and intelligent process**. The path to a powerful predictive model does not lie in accumulating the maximum number of features, but in the methodical distillation of the most potent information.

The brute-force "inverse selection" strategy mistakes quantity of computation for quality of insight. Our four-stage pipeline embodies the opposite philosophy. It recognizes that in a domain saturated with noise, the modeler's primary task is to impose order, enforce parsimony, and guide the learning process toward robust, generalizable patterns. By embracing this discipline, we move beyond the allure of complexity and build models that are not only statistically sound but also interpretable, efficient, and better equipped to navigate the enduring complexities of financial markets.

Chapter 10: The "State-Snapshot" Model: A Non-Recursive Approach to Financial Prediction

10.1 Introduction: Redefining Temporal Dependence in Financial Models

In the domain of time-series forecasting, a dominant paradigm involves explicitly modeling temporal sequences. Models such as ARIMA and Recurrent Neural Networks (RNNs) are designed to process inputs as a sequence of past observations (e.g., values at time $t-1, t-2, \dots, t-n$) to predict the state at time $t+1$. This approach assumes that the "memory" of the system is best captured by feeding the raw historical sequence directly into the model.

This chapter explores a powerful alternative paradigm, which is the one implemented in our codebase. Instead of explicitly modeling the past, our approach **implicitly models history** by using only a "state-snapshot" of the market at time t. We operate under the thesis that a well-chosen vector of technical indicators at the present moment provides a sufficiently rich, condensed summary of the relevant past, making the use of explicit lagged values redundant and often counterproductive.

We will deconstruct the rationale behind this non-recursive methodology, examining how technical indicators function as convolutions of market history, and analyzing the profound benefits this approach offers in terms of dimensionality reduction, noise filtering, and mitigating the challenges of non-stationarity inherent in financial markets.

10.2 Technical Indicators as Convolutions of Market History

The core justification for the state-snapshot approach lies in a deep understanding of what a technical indicator truly represents. An indicator is not merely a number; it is a **feature extractor** that performs a mathematical convolution over a window of past price data, transforming a high-dimensional price history into a single, meaningful value.

Consider these examples:

- **Simple Moving Average (SMA):** The current value of a 20-period SMA is the literal average of the last 20 closing prices. It is a mathematical summary of that entire price window.

- **Relative Strength Index (RSI):** The current 14-period RSI value is a more complex function, but it is still derived entirely from the sequence of upward and downward price changes over the last 14 periods.

- **Average Directional Index (ADX):** An ADX(21) value encapsulates 21 periods of high, low, and close data to produce a single number representing trend strength.

Therefore, when our model receives a feature vector at time t, such as:

$$F(t)=[CCI\_14(t),ADX\_21(t),ATR\_21(t),\ldots]$$

It is not just seeing the present. It is implicitly being fed a rich, pre-processed, and condensed summary of the market's behavior over the last 14 and 21 periods. Our model does not ignore the past; it simply trusts these sophisticated indicators to have already extracted the relevant historical context.

10.3 The Rationale: Why This Approach is Suited for Financial Markets

Choosing this state-snapshot methodology over a sequence-based one is a deliberate engineering decision designed to address the unique challenges of financial data.

a. Dimensionality Reduction and Noise Filtering

Using a sequence of raw past prices as input (e.g., the last 50 closing prices) creates an extremely high-dimensional and noisy feature space. The model must learn to distinguish meaningful patterns from a sea of high-frequency noise, a task that dramatically increases the risk of overfitting.

Technical indicators, by their very nature, act as **intelligent dimensionality reduction and noise filtering mechanisms**. An indicator like an EMA smooths out volatile price action, allowing the model to focus on the underlying trend rather than on ephemeral price spikes. By using a handful of indicators, we transform a noisy, high-dimensional history into a clean, low-dimensional vector of meaningful concepts (e.g., "momentum," "trend," "volatility"), making the learning task for our classification model substantially easier and more robust.

b. Mitigating Non-Stationarity

A critical challenge in financial modeling is that price series are **non-stationary**; their statistical properties, such as mean and variance, change over time. A stock trading at \$10 in 2010 and \$200 in 2025 operates in completely different statistical regimes. Many machine learning models struggle with non-stationary inputs.

Many technical indicators, however, are specifically designed to be more stationary. Oscillators like the **RSI** and **Stochastic Oscillator** are mathematically bounded (e.g., between 0 and 100). They measure the *relative* position of the current price within a recent range, a concept that remains valid whether the price is \$10 or \$200. By feeding the model these more stationary, normalized inputs, we create a more stable learning environment, leading to models that can generalize better across different price regimes and time periods.

c. Simplicity and the Bias-Variance Tradeoff

As discussed in the previous chapter, a core challenge is managing the bias-variance tradeoff.

- A **complex sequence model (like an LSTM)** has very low bias (it has the capacity to learn intricate temporal patterns) but extremely high variance (it is notoriously difficult to train and highly prone to overfitting the specific sequences in the training data).

- Our **state-snapshot model** makes a strategic trade-off. We introduce a modest amount of bias by assuming that our vector of indicators is a *sufficient summary* of the relevant past. In exchange, we achieve a dramatic reduction in model variance. By simplifying the input structure, we make it much harder for the model to overfit, leading to more robust and reliable generalization. In a domain where the signal-to-noise ratio is low, this is often a winning tradeoff.

10.4 A Critical Comparison: State-Snapshot vs. Sequence Models

The choice of modeling paradigm is not a matter of one being universally "better," but of selecting the right tool for the job.

Aspect	State-Snapshot Model (Agnostic Approach)	Sequence Model (e.g., LSTM/RNN)
Input Structure	A single vector of features at time t: F(t)	A sequence (tensor) of feature vectors: [F(t), F(t-1), ...]
Historical View	**Implicit:** History is condensed into the indicator values.	**Explicit:** The model directly processes the historical sequence.
Pros	Computationally efficient and fast. Simpler architecture, easier to implement and debug. Less prone to overfitting temporal noise. More interpretable feature importance.	Theoretically can capture very long-term dependencies. Can model the "grammar" or syntax of market movements.
Cons	Inherits the intrinsic lag of its indicators. Cannot model patterns that span longer than the lookback window of its slowest indicator.	Extremely high data and computational requirements. Notoriously difficult to train and tune. Very high risk of overfitting. "Black box" nature makes it difficult to interpret.

Our choice of the state-snapshot model is a pragmatic one. It is exceptionally well-suited for capturing local market dynamics based on well-established financial concepts, without the immense complexity and data hunger of true sequence-to-sequence models.

10.5 Conclusion: The Power of an Implicit Historical View

By training a model using only the current values of technical indicators, our methodology deliberately departs from more complex, recursive approaches. This framework is not "ahistorical" or ignorant of the past. On the contrary, it leverages technical indicators as sophisticated feature extractors, each providing a rich, condensed summary of market history from a different perspective—be it trend, momentum, or volatility.

This design choice provides a powerful trifecta of benefits perfectly suited to the financial domain: **robustness**, **efficiency**, and **interpretability**. It yields simpler models that are less prone to overfitting noise, faster to train and deploy, and whose decisions can be more readily understood. While it forgoes the ability to model very long-term temporal dependencies, its effectiveness demonstrates that for many practical forecasting tasks, a well-curated snapshot of the present market state contains sufficient information to make a robust, high-probability prediction of the near future.

Chapter 11: A Principled and Real Agnostic Data-Driven Methodology: Letting the Evidence Speak

11.1 Introduction: From Naïve Agnosticism to a Structured Dialogue with Data

The maxim to "let the data speak" is a foundational principle of empirical science. In machine learning, however, its interpretation is critical. A naïve interpretation might suggest a posture of complete agnosticism, where one abdicates all structural assumptions and resorts to a brute-force, exhaustive search of every conceivable model and feature combination. This approach, while appearing unbiased, is statistically perilous. It creates a scenario of near-infinite multiple testing, where the probability of discovering spurious correlations and producing a dangerously overfit model approaches certainty. It is not a dialogue with the data; it is an interrogation under duress, where the data will eventually confess to anything if tortured enough.

This chapter details a more sophisticated paradigm implemented by our code. It reframes "letting the data speak" as a **structured, Socratic dialogue**. We do not make a priori assumptions about which specific model or feature is "best," but we impose a rigorous, hierarchical process of inquiry. This framework is designed to ask a series of progressively more specific questions, using the evidence from one stage to intelligently inform the questions of the next. It is a methodology built on the understanding that a meaningful answer can only be obtained by asking a well-posed question.

11.2 The Nuanced Role of Agnosticism in Our Pipeline

Our framework's power derives from its strategic application of agnosticism. It is agnostic about outcomes but dogmatic about process.

a. Architectural Agnosticism: Diagnosing the Nature of the Problem

The **"Model Horse Race"** of Stage 2 is the primary application of our agnosticism. We present the data with a diverse portfolio of learning architectures, each possessing a distinct **inductive bias**—a set of core assumptions about the nature of the solution.

- **Linear Models (LogisticRegression):** Assume the boundary between classes is best approximated by a straight line (or hyperplane) in the feature space. They test the hypothesis: "Is the predictive signal fundamentally additive and linear?"

- **Tree-Ensemble Models (RandomForest, XGBoost):** Assume the solution lies in a complex, hierarchical set of rules and interactions. They test the hypothesis: "Is the signal interactive and non-linear, requiring the feature space to be partitioned into many local regions?"

- **Instance-Based Models (KNeighborsClassifier):** Assume that similar data points in the feature space lead to similar outcomes. They test the hypothesis: "Is the signal local and based on proximity, without a global underlying function?"

By evaluating these competing hypotheses fairly under cross-validation, we do more than just pick a "winner." We perform a powerful diagnostic test on our data itself. A strong performance from tree ensembles, for example, provides compelling evidence that the underlying market dynamics we seek to model are inherently non-linear and interactive.

b. Feature Agnosticism: From Human Intuition to Statistical Relevance

Rather than relying on the "folk wisdom" of trading literature or a trader's personal biases about favorite indicators, our process begins with a principled agnosticism towards features. In **Stage 1**, we use **Mutual Information** to score our features. This information-theoretic measure is superior to simple correlation because it captures any kind of statistical dependency, including non-linear ones. It objectively quantifies how much uncertainty about the Target is reduced by knowing the value of a feature. This allows the data, through the lens of robust statistics, to tell us which features are most relevant, freeing us from narrative-based or intuitive biases that may be suboptimal.

11.3 Implementing an Evidence-Based Funnel: A Deeper Look

Our code operationalizes this philosophy by treating the modeling pipeline as a formal process of evidence accumulation.

- **Stage 1: Evidence from Foundational Statistics** The compute_feature_selection function acts as a stringent statistical gatekeeper. The evidence required for a feature to pass this stage is not its performance in a model, but its intrinsic statistical properties. We demand evidence of **information content** (non-zero variance), **relevance** (high mutual information with the target), and **novelty** (low correlation with other selected features). The latter is critical for mitigating **multicollinearity**, a statistical condition where predictors are inter-correlated. High multicollinearity can make a model's learned parameters highly unstable and its feature importance metrics unreliable, obscuring the true drivers of its predictions. Our process prunes this redundancy from the outset.

- **Stage 2: Evidence from Cross-Validated Performance** The evidence gathered in the horse race is a significant step up in quality. We assess not just raw performance, but **robustness to data variation**. By using **k-fold cross-validation**, we train and test each model five times on different subsets of the training data. A model that performs well on only one fold but poorly on others is fragile. A model that achieves a high average score across all folds provides strong evidence that its performance is not a fluke, but a reflection of its ability to generalize across different data samples. This is our primary mechanism for estimating a model's **generalization error** and selecting for stability.

- **Stage 3: Evidence from Hyperparameter Optimization** The tune_best_models function is an exercise in navigating a model's internal **complexity space**. Hyperparameters like max_depth in a decision tree or C in an SVM directly control the model's capacity to fit the data, governing its position on the bias-variance spectrum. GridSearchCV provides evidence for which configuration finds the optimal balance. By systematically testing these "dials" and using cross-validation, we find the hyperparameter set that is most robust, ensuring we are not just choosing a powerful architecture, but its most stable and effective configuration.

- **Stage 4: The Ultimate Evidence from a Pristine Test Set** The final backtest is the ultimate arbiter. The test set is **"out-of-sample" and "out-of-process."** It has played no role in feature selection, model selection, or hyperparameter tuning. It represents our one and only opportunity to simulate a true encounter with the future. The performance on this set is the most unbiased estimate of the model's real-world potential. Even this, however, should be viewed with professional humility, as the future will always present new data that is potentially "out-of-distribution" compared to our historical sample.

11.4 A Framework for Avoiding Cognitive and Statistical Biases

This structured process is an engineered defense against the biases that plague quantitative research.

- **Confirmation Bias:** The pipeline forces objectivity. An analyst might believe strongly in SVMs, but if the horse race consistently shows that tree-based ensembles are superior for a given dataset, the evidence compels a change in direction. The process forces us to confront and act on the data's emergent properties, rather than our own preconceptions.

- **Overfitting:** By explicitly rejecting the combinatorial explosion of the "inverse selection" method, we directly attack the primary cause of overfitting. Our funnel curtails the model's "degrees of freedom" at each stage, not by limiting its learning capacity, but by constraining the search space to the most promising avenues. This discipline is our most potent defense against learning the noise instead of the signal.

11.5 Conclusion: Trusting the Process, Validating the Outcome

Ultimately, the philosophy embodied in this code is a transition from trusting intuition to trusting a **process**. The goal is not to stumble upon a single "magic" model that will work forever, but rather to build a reliable **"factory" for producing models**. This framework is a robust, repeatable, and defensible scientific instrument for interrogating the market.

It acknowledges that "letting the data speak" is not a passive act of listening to a chaotic cacophony. It is an active, structured dialogue where we ask intelligent questions, demand robust evidence, and build our conclusions on a foundation of statistical rigor. The final model is not chosen because it was our favorite, or because it produced a single spectacular result in a sea of tests. It is chosen because it is the validated survivor of a hierarchical gauntlet designed to separate true predictive signal from the seductive allure of random chance.

Chapter 12: From Heuristics to Probabilities: A Model-Based Decision Framework

12.1 Introduction: Shifting from "Rules" to "Learned Functions"

One of the most profound shifts offered by a machine learning approach is the evolution from human-defined trading rules to data-driven, model-guided decisions. A traditional discretionary or rule-based trader operates on a set of explicit heuristics: "If the RSI is below 30 and the price crosses the 50-day moving average, then buy." These rules are born from experience and analysis but are inherently static and limited by the human capacity to define them.

The methodology implemented in our code takes a fundamentally different path. It does not contain a single if/then rule for trade entry. Instead, the core of our system is a single, powerful, data-derived decision function:

Prediction=f(Feature1,Feature2,...,FeatureN)

This function, which is our trained machine learning model, learns the complex, non-linear relationships between market indicators and the probability of a future price increase or decrease. This chapter explores the anatomy of this model-based decision, clarifies the "black box" concept within our disciplined framework, and redefines the role of the trader from a rule-follower to a system architect.

12.2 The Anatomy of a Model-Based Decision

To understand how our system operates, it is crucial to recognize that the live trading bot is an **execution engine**, not a learning engine. The "intelligence"—the feature selection, model selection, and tuning—has already been created during the rigorous, **offline training pipeline** described in the previous chapters.

a. A Pre-Defined, Validated System

Contrary to a system that might dynamically test different features or models in real-time, our approach is based on deploying a static, pre-vetted artifact. The entire four-stage pipeline is run offline to produce a single **champion model** for a specific market session (e.g., for the 13:00 hour). This champion is a complete, self-contained Pipeline object, saved as a .pkl file, that already "knows" which features to use, how to scale them, and which hyperparameters are optimal. The live trading bot's only job is to load this artifact and feed it current market data.

b. The Input: A "State-Snapshot" of the Market

As established in Chapter 10, the model's entire perception of the market at any given moment is the **state-snapshot**: a single vector containing the current values of its pre-defined features (e.g., [CCI_value, ADX_value, ATR_value]).

c. The Transformation: Inside the "Translucent Box"

When the live bot calls pipeline.predict(), a two-step process occurs:

1. **Preprocessing:** The input data vector is passed to the StandardScaler saved within the pipeline, which normalizes the data using the parameters (mean and standard deviation) learned *from the training set*. This ensures that the live data is transformed in a way that is perfectly consistent with the training data.

2. **Classification:** The scaled data is then passed to the trained classifier (e.g., the tuned XGBoost model). This model is, at its core, a complex mathematical function. While we cannot easily write out the thousands of decision rules within a large ensemble of trees, its behavior is not a complete mystery. We know precisely what it was trained on and what objective it was optimized for.

d. The Output: A Calculated Probability

Crucially, the model's raw output is not just a "BUY" or "SELL" command. It is a **probability**. For a given state-snapshot, the model might output [0.25, 0.75], signifying a 25% probability of the "SELL" class (Target=0) and a 75% probability of the "BUY" class (Target=1). Our live trading code then applies a threshold (e.g., probability > 0.53) to this output to make the final, discrete trade decision. This transforms trading from a binary, rule-based activity into a more nuanced, probability-driven one.

12.3 De-Mystifying the "Black Box": Why We Can Trust the Model

The term "black box" often implies a lack of control or understanding. However, in our framework, we can have a high degree of confidence in the model's decisions, not because we can interpret every internal calculation, but because we have immense trust in the **process used to create it.**

- **Trust Through Process:** Our trust is not blind. It is earned through the rigorous, multi-stage validation pipeline. We trust the model because it is the survivor of a gauntlet: it was built from statistically relevant features, it won a fair competition against other architectures, it was fine-tuned for robustness, and it was validated on unseen data. Our confidence is in the integrity of this process.

- **Objectivity and Emotional Discipline:** This remains one of the greatest strengths of a model-based approach. The model is immune to fear, greed, or the "fear of missing out" (FOMO). It executes its learned statistical edge with perfect discipline, every single time. It acts as an automated tool for enforcing the strategy we so painstakingly validated.

- **Adaptability Through Retraining:** The system's adaptability does not come from dynamically switching models in real-time. Instead, it comes from the ability to periodically **re-run the entire training pipeline** on more recent data. As market conditions evolve over months or years, we can generate a new champion model that is adapted to the new reality. Adaptability lies in the framework, not in the deployed model itself.

- **Handling Complexity Intelligently:** The model's strength is not in processing thousands of features, but in its ability to find complex, non-linear relationships *within the minimal, curated set of features* we provide. It can detect synergies and patterns that are too subtle for the human eye or simple rule-based systems, all while being constrained to a feature space that we have already validated as robust and meaningful.

12.4 Conclusion: The Trader as a Systems Architect

This data-driven paradigm fundamentally redefines the role of the quantitative trader. The trader is no longer a "signal spotter" or a "rule follower." Instead, the trader becomes a **systems architect and manager**.

The primary responsibilities shift from making individual trade decisions to a higher level of oversight:

1. **Designing and Maintaining the Data Pipeline:** Ensuring the data used for training is clean, accurate, and consistent with live data.

2. **Architecting the Experimental Framework:** Defining and refining the four-stage validation pipeline to ensure its statistical robustness.

3. **Monitoring and Evaluating Live Performance:** Continuously tracking the model's live PnL and performance metrics to detect any degradation or deviation from backtested expectations.

4. **Governing the Retraining Cycle:** Deciding when the evidence suggests that market conditions have changed enough to warrant retraining the model and deploying an updated version.

By embracing this approach, we are not ceding control to an unknowable black box. We are leveraging a powerful, probability-based tool that we have meticulously built and validated. We trust it to execute the complex patterns it has learned, freeing us to focus on the strategic oversight and continuous improvement of the entire trading system.

Chapter 13: Engineering Antifragile Systems: Robustness and Principled Agnosticism in Financial Markets

13.1 Introduction: The Problem of Induction and the Quest for Antifragility

At the heart of all predictive endeavors lies the philosophical challenge known as the **Problem of Induction**: the profound uncertainty that arises from using past observations to make claims about the future. This is nowhere more acute than in financial markets—complex, adaptive systems characterized by non-stationarity and epistemic opacity. A model trained on the past is, by definition, unprepared for a future that does not precisely resemble it.

It is in this context that Nassim Nicholas Taleb's concept of **antifragility** becomes not just a compelling idea, but a necessary design principle. To build systems that can navigate such inherent uncertainty, we must understand the fundamental triad of responses to volatility and disorder:

- **The Fragile:** That which shatters under stress, randomness, and shock. A wine glass is fragile. In modeling, a heavily overfit strategy that relies on a single, unstable market correlation is exceedingly fragile.

- **The Robust (or Resilient):** That which withstands stress and remains unchanged. A stone is robust. A well-hedged, low-volatility portfolio is robust. It endures chaos but does not improve from it.

- **The Antifragile:** That which *gains* from stress, randomness, and shock. In mythology, the Hydra, which grew two new heads for each one severed, was antifragile. In finance, certain options strategies that deliver explosive payoffs during market panics are antifragile. They feed on disorder.

While creating a single predictive model that is purely antifragile is a near-impossibility—as models are optimized for a specific expected outcome—we can and must engineer a **development process** that exhibits antifragile properties. This chapter provides a deep dive into how our structured, four-stage pipeline is fundamentally a framework for identifying and eliminating sources of fragility, thereby building models that are exceptionally robust and are the product of a system that learns and improves from market complexity.

13.2 Identifying the Sources of Model Fragility

To build a resilient system, we must first be ruthless in identifying its potential points of failure. For a machine learning model in finance, fragility stems primarily from two sources: the model's internal structure and the process used to create it.

a. Model-Based Fragility: The Brittleness of Overfitting

Overfitting is the principal source of model fragility. An overfit model has not learned the underlying, persistent signal in the data; it has memorized the idiosyncratic noise of its training sample. It is a "brittle lattice of assumptions," perfectly calibrated to a historical regime that is gone forever. When faced with new data, which inevitably contains different noise, this brittle structure shatters. Its failure is not graceful; it is catastrophic. A model that seemed to have a 70% accuracy in backtesting may perform no better than a random coin flip in live trading, precisely because its perceived "edge" was an illusion born from overfitting.

b. Process-Based Fragility: The Danger of Flawed Methodology

A fragile process will invariably produce a fragile model. A methodology is fragile if it contains structural weaknesses that invite spurious results. Key process-based fragilities include:

- **Data Leakage:** Allowing information from the future (e.g., the test set) to contaminate the training process, giving the model an unrealistic and unrepeatable advantage.

- **Inappropriate Metrics:** Using naïve metrics like accuracy on an imbalanced dataset can lead to the selection of a useless model that simply predicts the majority class.

- **Data Dredging:** The brute-force "inverse selection" approach is a textbook example of a fragile process. By testing an exponential number of combinations, it maximizes the odds of finding a "lucky" model, making the entire selection process fragile to the specific random sample of data used for training.

Our pipeline is engineered to systematically eliminate these fragilities at every stage.

13.3 How Our Pipeline Engineers Robustness: A Step-by-Step Deconstruction

Our framework builds robustness methodically, ensuring the final model is the result of a process that has been stress-tested from start to finish.

1. **Stage 1 - Building a Robust Informational Foundation:** A model is only as strong as its inputs. A model fed with noisy, redundant, and irrelevant features is inherently fragile, as it relies on unstable statistical relationships. The compute_feature_selection function acts as a fortification process. By filtering based on variance, relevance (Mutual Information), and redundancy (correlation), it creates a stable, high-signal representation of the market state. This makes the model's inputs themselves more robust to random market chatter.

2. **Stage 2 - Selecting for Architectural Resilience:** A model is fragile if its core architecture (its inductive bias) is a poor match for the problem's structure. The "Model Horse Race" is a diagnostic test to prevent this mismatch. By forcing diverse architectures—linear, tree-based, instance-based—to compete on a level playing field, we

85

select the model family whose fundamental assumptions best align with the data's character, ensuring architectural resilience.

3. **Stages 3 & 4 - Quantifying Robustness Through Adversarial Validation:** A model whose quality is judged on a single, favorable data split is fragile. Our pipeline's use of **cross-validation** (in GridSearchCV) and a **pristine hold-out test set** represents a form of adversarial testing. We actively challenge the model to prove its performance is consistent across different data subsets. A model that endures this process provides powerful evidence of its robustness. It has been stressed, tested, and validated, hardening it against the fragility of statistical flukes.

13.4 The Barbell Strategy: A Precise Metaphor for Our Development Process

The most accurate and powerful analogy for our pipeline's philosophy is Taleb's **Barbell Strategy**. This strategy advocates for avoiding the "mediocre middle" and instead partitioning resources between two extremes: a large allocation to assets of maximum safety and a small allocation to assets of maximum speculation. This creates a system that is protected from ruin but remains open to unlimited positive surprises. Our development process is a direct implementation of this concept.

- **The "Safe" End of the Barbell (90% of our methodology): The Bedrock of Disciplined Process** This is the core of our framework, our "Treasury bonds" that protect us from catastrophic failure (i.e., deploying a worthless, overfit model). This safe allocation consists of our non-negotiable principles:

    1. **The Scientific Method:** A structured, hierarchical process of inquiry.

    2. **Rigorous Data Segregation:** The absolute sanctity of the test set.

    3. **Statistical Feature Filtering:** The use of compute_feature_selection to build a robust foundation.

    4. **Robust Metrics:** The deliberate choice of f1_weighted over simple accuracy.

    5. **Cross-Validation:** The mandate to use cross-validation at every evaluation step (cross_val_score, GridSearchCV).

- **The "Speculative" End of the Barbell (10% of our methodology): Controlled Exploration** This is our "venture capital" allocation, where we take small, calculated risks to expose ourselves to massive positive upside. This includes:

    1. **Casting a Wide Architectural Net:** Including a diverse range of models in the MODELS list for the horse race. We might discover that for a particular market regime, an unconventional model like KNeighborsClassifier dramatically outperforms the usual suspects.

86

2. **Exploring the Edges of Hyperparameter Space:** Defining a broad PARAM_GRIDS for GridSearchCV. While most of the tested combinations will not be optimal, one particular setting might unlock a new level of performance, providing a significant "payout."

This barbell design ensures our process is fundamentally safe but not stagnant. It protects us from ruin while ensuring we are always open to discovering novel, high-performing solutions.

13.5 Conclusion: The Antifragile Research System

In the final analysis, our objective is not to create a single, magically antifragile *model*. Such an entity is likely a theoretical impossibility.

Instead, we have built something far more valuable: an **antifragile *system for generating and validating models***.

This system—our entire Python script and the methodology it embodies—is what gains from disorder. When a market shock occurs or a new regime emerges, the currently deployed model may see its performance degrade. This is a stress event. However, the "factory" itself does not break. The new, chaotic market data is not a threat; it is valuable new information. We can feed this new data into our robust, barbell-inspired pipeline and re-run the process. The factory will then produce a *new champion model*, one that has learned from the recent disorder and is now better adapted to the new market reality.

The system learns from its mistakes and grows stronger from market volatility. It is a process that turns stressors into improvements. This is the very definition of antifragility, applied not to a single prediction, but to the entire research and development lifecycle.

Chapter 14: The Exploration-Exploitation Cycle in Model Development and Deployment

14.1 The Fundamental Dilemma: To Search or to Profit?

A central challenge in any adaptive system is managing the **exploration-exploitation trade-off**. This dilemma represents a constant tension between two competing priorities:

- **Exploration:** The act of searching, experimenting, and gathering new information. It involves testing new strategies, models, or feature combinations with the goal of discovering a solution that is superior to the current best. Exploration is an investment in the future, but it comes at the cost of forgoing a guaranteed short-term outcome.

- **Exploitation:** The act of using the best-known strategy to maximize performance based on current knowledge. It involves capitalizing on a proven edge to achieve immediate results. Exploitation is profitable in the short-term, but a system that only ever exploits will never discover better strategies and risks becoming obsolete as its environment changes.

In financial markets, this translates to the choice between continuing to use a proven, profitable strategy (exploitation) versus dedicating resources to research and test new strategies that might perform even better or adapt to new market conditions (exploration).

14.2 A Methodical Separation: How Our Pipeline Manages the Trade-Off

Many advanced systems attempt to solve this dilemma in real-time. Our framework, however, adopts a more deliberate, practical, and robust approach by **separating the lifecycle into distinct offline and online phases.** Our system does not automatically rebalance; instead, it provides the tools for a human architect to govern the cycle intelligently.

a. The "Exploration" Phase: The Offline Training Pipeline

The entirety of the script we have built for training, selection, and validation represents one comprehensive, exhaustive **exploration phase**. During this offline process, the system is purely dedicated to discovery.

- **Exploring Features:** In Stage 1, it explores the initial feature pool to find a statistically robust subset.

- **Exploring Architectures:** In Stage 2, it explores a wide variety of model families to identify the most suitable inductive bias.

- **Exploring Parameters:** In Stage 3, it explores a vast space of hyperparameters to optimize the winning architectures.

The singular goal of running this entire script is to conclude the exploration phase by identifying the single best strategy (the champion model) based on all available historical data.

b. The "Exploitation" Phase: Live Model Deployment

Once the exploration phase is complete and a champion model has been saved as a .pkl file, the system transitions entirely to the **exploitation phase**.

- The live trading bot is a pure exploitation engine. It does not learn, explore, or adapt in real-time.

- Its sole function is to execute the "best-known strategy" discovered during the offline exploration. It repeatedly applies this static, pre-validated mathematical function to live market data to generate trading signals.

- This ensures that our live performance is based on a rigorously validated model, free from the unpredictability of an online learning system that might alter its strategy erratically.

14.3 Managing the Cycle: The Human-in-the-Loop Feedback System

If the deployed model only ever exploits, how does the system adapt to changing markets? The answer lies in a crucial feedback loop that is governed not by an algorithm, but by a **strategic, human-in-the-loop decision.**

- **The Feedback Loop:** The "feedback" is the ongoing monitoring of the live model's performance (its PnL, drawdown, accuracy, etc.). This data tells us how well our "exploited" knowledge is holding up against new market realities.

- **The Trigger for Re-Exploration:** When we observe that the live model's performance is degrading over time—a phenomenon known as **alpha decay** or **concept drift**—this negative feedback serves as a trigger. It signals that our current "best-known strategy" is becoming stale.

- **The Decision:** At this point, the system architect (the trader or quant) makes the strategic decision to end the current exploitation phase and initiate a new exploration phase. This means re-running the entire offline training pipeline, often on an updated dataset that includes the most recent market data.

This cycle of offline exploration followed by online exploitation, governed by performance monitoring, is a robust and practical solution to the dilemma. It provides stability during exploitation while ensuring long-term adaptability through periodic, data-driven retraining.

14.4 The Synergy with Antifragility and the Barbell Strategy

This deliberate management of the exploration-exploitation cycle is deeply connected to the principles of building an antifragile system.

- **Antifragility Through Adaptation:** A system that cannot adapt to change is fragile. Our framework builds antifragility by establishing a clear process for adaptation. The "stress" of a model's performance degradation in a new market regime does not cause the system to break; it is the very event that **triggers the process of renewal and improvement**. The system uses this failure as an opportunity to learn from the new market data, explore new solutions, and emerge with a stronger, better-adapted model. It gains from disorder over the long run.

- **The Barbell Analogy Revisited:** This cycle can also be viewed through the lens of the Barbell Strategy:

    - **Exploitation (The Safe End):** The period of live trading with the champion model is like living off the steady returns of our "safe assets." We are exploiting a known, validated edge with a predictable risk profile.

    - **Exploration (The Speculative End):** The act of dedicating time and computational resources to re-running the entire training pipeline is our "speculative bet." We invest resources in a high-upside endeavor—the possibility of discovering a new, more profitable model. The potential "payout" is a new source of alpha. The "risk" is the computational cost, which is controlled and deliberate.

14.5 Conclusion: A Disciplined Cycle of Discovery and Execution

The exploration-exploitation dilemma is a fundamental challenge in any learning system. Rather than attempting to solve it with a single, complex, real-time algorithm, our methodology provides a clear, disciplined, and practical solution by separating the two tasks into distinct phases.

The system dedicates itself to an intense, structured period of **offline exploration** to discover the most robust possible strategy. It then transitions to a disciplined period of **online exploitation**, where that strategy is executed with precision. The cycle renews not automatically, but through the crucial oversight of a human architect who monitors performance and decides when the evidence warrants a return to the exploratory phase.

This cyclical approach creates a system that is both stable in the short term and highly adaptive in the long term. It embodies a mature solution to the trade-off, ensuring that our trading framework is in a constant, managed state of evolution, forever balancing the need to profit from current knowledge with the essential quest to discover the knowledge of tomorrow.

Chapter 15: Advanced Horizons: Reinforcement Learning and the Future of Adaptive Trading

15.1 Introduction: Beyond Supervised Prediction

The preceding chapters have meticulously detailed a robust pipeline for developing predictive models using **supervised learning**. In that paradigm, we train a model on a historical dataset with predefined features (X) and clear, correct labels (y), teaching it to map inputs to a probabilistic outcome. The cycle of exploration and exploitation, as we discussed, is a strategic, human-governed process of offline training and online deployment.

We now turn our attention to a more advanced and fundamentally different paradigm: **Reinforcement Learning (RL)**. RL is not concerned with predicting a static label but with teaching an autonomous "agent" to make an optimal sequence of decisions in a dynamic environment to maximize a cumulative reward.

This chapter will introduce the core concepts of Reinforcement Learning and explore how it represents a potential future evolution for our trading system. We will examine how RL naturally and automatically manages the exploration-exploitation trade-off and discuss both its immense potential and the significant challenges associated with its application in the complex, noisy environment of financial markets.

15.2 The Core Concepts of Reinforcement Learning

Reinforcement Learning is a paradigm in which an agent learns by continuously interacting with an environment. This process of trial and error, guided by feedback, allows the agent to develop a sophisticated strategy, or "policy," over time.

The key components of RL are:

- **Agent:** The decision-maker. In our context, this would be the trading algorithm itself.

- **Environment:** The world in which the agent operates. For us, this is the financial market.

- **State (S):** A snapshot of the environment at a given moment. This is analogous to our feature vector (e.g., the current values of CCI, ADX, ATR).

- **Action (A):** A decision the agent can make. Instead of just a binary prediction, this could be a richer set of actions like BUY, SELL, HOLD, INCREASE POSITION, or DECREASE POSITION.

- **Reward (R):** The feedback from the environment after an action. This is the most critical component—it could be the immediate profit or loss from a trade, a risk-adjusted return like the Sharpe ratio, or a penalty for excessive drawdown.

- **Policy (π):** The agent's strategy. The policy is a function that maps a given state to a specific action, defining the agent's behavior. The goal of RL is to find the optimal policy, $\pi*$.

In essence, an RL agent for trading would learn a policy that tells it the best action to take (buy, sell, hold, etc.) for any given set of market indicators, with the goal of maximizing its long-term, risk-adjusted profit.

15.3 The RL Solution to the Exploration-Exploitation Dilemma

Chapter 14 described our human-governed cycle of offline exploration (training) and online exploitation (trading). Reinforcement Learning addresses this dilemma differently, integrating it directly and automatically into the agent's learning process.

- **Exploration in RL:** The agent must actively try actions that it doesn't currently believe are optimal. It might, for instance, take a "SELL" action in a state where its current policy suggests "HOLD," simply to gather information about the outcome. This is essential for discovering new, potentially more profitable strategies that would otherwise be missed. This is managed algorithmically through techniques like an **epsilon-greedy strategy**, where the agent takes a random action with a small probability, $\square$.

- **Exploitation in RL:** Most of the time, the agent will exploit its current knowledge by choosing the action that its learned policy identifies as having the highest expected future reward.

An RL agent is in a constant, dynamic dance between these two modes. It continuously uses the feedback from its exploratory actions to update and improve its core strategy, aiming to converge on a highly optimal policy over time.

15.4 Contrasting Our Supervised Pipeline with a Potential RL System

It is vital to understand that the robust pipeline we have built is not an RL system. They are two distinct approaches to the same problem, each with its own strengths and complexities.

Aspect	Supervised Learning Pipeline (Our Current Code)	Reinforcement Learning System (A Future Goal)

	Predictive Mapping: Learns a function f(X) -> y. It predicts the probability of a predefined event (e.g., price going up).	Policy Optimization: Learns a policy π(S) -> A. It learns a sequence of actions to maximize a cumulative reward.
Learning Task	Predictive Mapping: Learns a function f(X) -> y. It predicts the probability of a predefined event (e.g., price going up).	Policy Optimization: Learns a policy π(S) -> A. It learns a sequence of actions to maximize a cumulative reward.
Decision-Making	The output is a **prediction**. A separate, human-defined logic layer decides to trade based on this prediction (e.g., if probability > 0.7, then BUY).	The output is an **action**. The agent itself decides whether to BUY, SELL, or HOLD as its direct output.
Exploration/Exploitation	**Offline & Human-Governed:** Exploration is the entire offline training/tuning process. Exploitation is the live deployment of the static model. The cycle is managed manually.	**Online & Algorithmic:** The agent automatically balances exploration and exploitation in real-time according to its algorithm (e.g., epsilon-greedy).
Data Requirement	A large, high-quality **labeled historical dataset** (X and y).	A high-fidelity **market simulator** for safe training, or the ability to learn directly from the live market (which is extremely risky and capital-intensive).
Core Challenge	Finding robust features and avoiding overfitting on a static dataset.	Designing a good reward function and managing the risks of real-time exploration.

Export to Sheets

15.5 The Significant Challenges of RL in Financial Markets

While RL is theoretically powerful, its application to finance is fraught with unique and substantial challenges that must be respected:

- **Reward Function Design:** This is arguably the hardest part. Is the goal pure profit? Or profit per unit of risk (Sharpe ratio)? How do you penalize large drawdowns or transaction costs? A poorly designed reward function can lead to an agent learning undesirable behaviors, such as taking on excessive hidden risks.

- **Extreme Non-Stationarity:** Financial markets are notoriously non-stationary. An RL agent trained during a low-volatility bull market may have its policy become completely obsolete and dangerous during a market crash. The agent must be able to recognize and adapt to these regime shifts.

- **The Peril of Live Exploration:** In a video game, the cost of a bad exploratory action is restarting a level. In finance, the cost is **real capital loss**. Allowing an agent to "explore" with real money is an exceptionally risky proposition, which is why a highly accurate market simulator is often a prerequisite for serious RL research in trading.

15.6 Conclusion: RL as the Next Frontier

Reinforcement Learning represents a true paradigm shift from the predictive modeling we have implemented. It is not a simple "add-on" but a complete re-architecting of the decision-making process.

Our current supervised learning pipeline is a robust, practical, and highly effective framework for building trading models. It excels at identifying high-probability setups based on historical data, and its separation of offline training from online execution makes it stable and understandable.

Reinforcement Learning offers a tantalizing glimpse into a more autonomous future, where an agent can learn and adapt its strategies dynamically. While its potential is immense, its complexity and challenges are equally significant. Therefore, RL should be viewed not as a replacement for our current methodology, but as the **next frontier**—a powerful and exciting area for advanced research and development, to be undertaken only after a solid foundation in robust, supervised predictive modeling has been thoroughly mastered.

Chapter 16: From Black Box to Glass Box: Interpretability in Our Supervised Learning Framework

16.1 The Challenge of Trust in a Model-Driven World

The robust, four-stage pipeline we have constructed is designed to produce a high-performance predictive model. Often, the "champion" models that emerge from this process are complex ensemble methods like XGBoost or RandomForest. While these models excel at capturing the intricate, non-linear dynamics of financial markets, they present a significant challenge: their internal decision-making processes can be opaque. This leads to the classic "black box" problem.

In a domain like financial trading—where decisions carry significant risk and where accountability is paramount—a lack of transparency is a major obstacle. Before deploying capital based on a model's output, stakeholders, risk managers, and regulators rightfully ask not just "What did the model predict?" but "*Why* did it make that prediction?" This chapter explores how we can address this challenge, moving from an opaque black box to an understandable "glass box" by leveraging both the inherent transparency of our development process and the power of modern Explainable AI (XAI) techniques.

16.2 Inherent Interpretability in Our Structured Pipeline

Before resorting to external tools, it is crucial to recognize that our four-stage methodology is intrinsically designed to build trust and transparency. We do not end up with a complete black box because our process provides layers of understanding at each step.

1. **Transparency of Inputs (Stage 1):** We know exactly what the model is looking at. The compute_feature_selection function provides us with a minimal, interpretable set of features. When the final model makes a decision, we know it is based on a well-understood set of concepts like ['CCI', 'ADX_21', 'ATR'], not on an inscrutable mix of 50 different indicators.

2. **Transparency of Architecture (Stage 2):** The "Model Horse Race" gives us insight into the nature of the problem. If ensemble methods consistently outperform linear models, it provides strong evidence that the underlying market dynamics are non-linear and interactive. This justifies the choice of a more complex model.

3. **Transparency of Behavior (Stage 4):** The disaggregated backtesting plots are a powerful form of behavioral interpretation. By examining the separate PnL curves for BUY and SELL opportunities, we can diagnose how the model behaves in different market conditions. For example, we might discover our model is an excellent bull market predictor but a poor bear market one, a critical insight for live deployment.

96

Our process ensures that even if the model's internal logic is complex, its inputs, architectural justification, and behavioral patterns are well-understood.

16.3 Peering Inside the Box: Applying Explainable AI (XAI)

While our process provides high-level transparency, Explainable AI (XAI) offers tools to probe the model's decision-making on a more granular level. These techniques can be applied directly to our saved champion model (.pkl file) to answer specific questions.

- **Feature Importance:** This is the most straightforward XAI technique. For tree-based models like RandomForest and XGBoost, we can easily extract and plot the feature importances. This shows which of our selected features the trained model relied on most heavily. It provides a clear ranking of the drivers behind the model's overall strategy.

- **LIME (Local Interpretable Model-agnostic Explanations):** LIME answers the question: "Why was *this specific prediction* made?" It works by creating a simple, interpretable model (like a linear model) that approximates the behavior of our complex black box model in the local vicinity of a single data point. For a specific trade in our backtest, LIME could tell us, "The model predicted BUY primarily because the ATR value was unusually high and the ADX_21 value was above 40."

- **SHAP (SHapley Additive exPlanations):** SHAP is a more sophisticated and theoretically sound method based on game theory. It calculates the precise contribution of each feature to a specific prediction, ensuring that the contributions sum up to the final output. SHAP values can provide rich, detailed visualizations showing not only *which* features were important for a trade, but also *how* they pushed the prediction towards "BUY" or "SELL."

By applying these XAI tools post-training, we can move from understanding the model's general behavior to explaining its specific, individual decisions.

16.4 Case Study: Explaining a Trade to Compliance

Let's revisit the scenario of a trading firm needing to justify a decision, but within the context of our supervised learning pipeline.

- **Scenario:** The firm's automated system, using a champion XGBoost model from our pipeline, executed a series of large BUY orders during a volatile market period. A compliance officer asks for a justification.

- **Challenge:** The team cannot simply point to a rule like "RSI was below 30." They need to explain the logic of their complex model.

- **Solution using our Framework and XAI:**

  1. **Process Explanation:** First, they present the entire four-stage validation pipeline report for that model, demonstrating that it was selected through a rigorous, objective process and showed strong, cross-validated performance on the f1_weighted metric.

  2. **Feature Importance:** They show the global feature importance plot for the champion model, which reveals that ATR (volatility) and ADX_21 (trend strength) are the two most influential features in its decision-making. This establishes that the model is designed to react to volatility and trend.

  3. **SHAP Analysis:** For the specific trades in question, they generate SHAP force plots. These plots clearly show that for each of those trades, a high and rising ATR value strongly pushed the prediction towards "BUY," while a strong ADX_21 value provided a secondary confirmation.

- **Outcome:** The firm can provide a comprehensive and defensible explanation. The decision was not arbitrary; it was the output of a rigorously validated model that is designed to identify high-momentum, high-volatility breakouts, and the specific market conditions at the time of the trade perfectly matched the patterns the model was trained to detect.

16.5 The Trade-Off Between Performance and Transparency

It is an enduring reality in machine learning that a trade-off often exists between a model's absolute predictive performance and its simplicity.

- A DecisionTreeClassifier with a depth of 3 is extremely interpretable; you can literally draw it on a whiteboard. However, it may not be powerful enough to capture market complexities.

- An XGBoost model with hundreds of trees is far more powerful but less interpretable.

Our framework helps manage this trade-off intelligently. The "Model Horse Race" in Stage 2 explicitly compares the performance of simpler models versus more complex ones. If a LogisticRegression model performs nearly as well as an XGBoost model, we are empowered to make a strategic choice. We could choose the slightly less performant but highly interpretable linear model, or we could choose the more powerful black box, now armed with the XAI tools needed to probe its behavior. This data-driven comparison allows us to make a conscious, informed decision about where to position ourselves on the performance-interpretability spectrum.

16.6 Conclusion: Building Trustworthy, High-Performance Systems

The "black box" problem is not an insurmountable barrier but a challenge to be managed with a sound process and the right tools. By abandoning the pursuit of a single, simple set of human-defined rules, we unlock the power of machine learning to detect complex patterns. We then manage the resulting complexity by:

1. **Using a rigorous, transparent validation framework** that builds confidence in the model's selection and overall behavior.

2. **Employing powerful XAI techniques** like SHAP and LIME to audit and explain the model's reasoning on a granular, per-decision basis.

This dual approach allows us to create trading systems that are not only high-performing but also accountable, understandable, and trustworthy—a critical combination for success in the modern financial industry.

Chapter 17: Modeling Market Regimes: A Time-Stratified Development Approach

17.1 Introduction: Time as a Primary Market Dimension

A foundational truth of financial markets is that they are not monolithic. The market at 03:00 GMT during the quiet Asian session is a fundamentally different environment from the market at 14:00 GMT during the high-volume, high-volatility overlap of the London and New York sessions. Liquidity, volatility, participant behavior, and the impact of news events all vary dramatically depending on the time of day.

A model that ignores this reality and attempts to apply a single, universal logic across all trading hours is likely to be mediocre at best. It will average out distinct market behaviors, failing to capture the unique patterns inherent in each session. Recognizing this, our pipeline's architecture introduces a final, powerful layer of analysis: **time stratification**.

This chapter explores how our script implements this concept by systematically building specialized models for each distinct segment of the trading day. Instead of building one "generalist" model, we build an "army of specialists," each one expertly trained for the unique conditions of its designated hour.

17.2 The Methodology: A Pipeline Within a Loop

The time-stratified approach is implemented through the outermost for loops in our script's main execution block:

```
1. # From the main execution block
2. for hour in range(0, 24):
3.    for minute in range(0, 60, minute_increment):
4.       print(f"\n{'='*20} PROCESSING: Hour={hour}, Minute={minute} {'='*20}")
5.
6.       # --- PREPARACIÓN DE DATOS ---
7.       df_full_segment = load_data(filepath, hour_filter=hour, minute_filter=minute)
8.
9.       # ... The ENTIRE 4-stage pipeline is executed from here...
10.
```

The logic is both simple and powerful:

1. **Isolate a Time Slice:** The loop first selects a specific slice of time from the master dataset (e.g., all data points that occurred between 13:00 and 13:59).

2. **Treat as a Unique Problem:** This data slice is treated as its own complete, standalone dataset, with its own unique statistical properties and patterns.

3. **Deploy the Full Pipeline:** The **entire four-stage pipeline**—from feature selection, through the model horse race, to hyperparameter tuning and final backtesting—is executed *from scratch* using only this time-specific data.

4. **Produce a Specialist Model:** The output of this process for each loop iteration is a champion model that is a **specialist**. It has been optimized with the single-minded purpose of understanding and predicting the market dynamics prevalent *only* during that specific hour.

This "pipeline within a loop" methodology ensures that we are not asking one model to master all market conditions, but rather asking 24 different models to each master one.

17.3 The Benefits of a Time-Stratified Approach

This strategy of building session-specific specialists offers several profound advantages over a one-size-fits-all model.

- **Capturing Session-Specific Dynamics:** It allows our models to learn patterns unique to each trading session. A model for the low-volatility Asian session might learn to identify mean-reverting patterns within a tight range. In contrast, a model for the London-New York overlap might excel at detecting high-momentum breakout signals. A generalist model would likely fail at both, as these two behaviors are contradictory.

- **Increased Model Simplicity and Focus:** By narrowing the scope of the problem for each model, we increase its chances of success. The model for the 14:00 hour does not need to concern itself with the dynamics of the 04:00 hour. This focused learning task means the model can often achieve high performance with a simpler feature set and architecture, further enhancing its robustness.

- **A Framework for "Time Agnosticism":** This approach embodies the most intelligent form of agnosticism regarding time. We do not assume that a strategy proven effective at 09:00 will be relevant at 15:00. We remain "agnostic" about which hour of the day holds the most profitable opportunities. By systematically deploying our robust pipeline to analyze each hour independently, we let the data from each session speak for itself and reveal its own unique, profitable patterns.

17.4 Encouraging Experimentation: The Dimension of Timeframes

While our code is configured to iterate through hours on a 60-minute timeframe (tf = 60), the framework is inherently flexible regarding the **timeframe** of the data itself. The tf parameter can be easily changed to allow for experimentation across different trading styles.

- **Shorter Timeframes (e.g., M15, M30):** Analyzing 15-minute or 30-minute candles would allow the models to focus on more granular, intraday price movements. This could be ideal for developing strategies that react more quickly to market shifts, especially during volatile periods.

- **Longer Timeframes (e.g., H4, D1):** For swing or position traders, analyzing 4-hour or daily candles would be more appropriate. This would allow the model to filter out short-term market noise and focus on capturing larger, more significant trends that evolve over days or weeks.

It is critical to note that changing the timeframe is a fundamental shift in the analysis. It would require generating a new master data file (e.g., EURUSD_15.csv from the data preparation script) and then re-running this entire training pipeline to build and validate a completely new set of models optimized for that specific resolution of time.

17.5 Conclusion: Building an Army of Specialists

The time-stratified methodology represents the final layer of sophistication in our modeling framework. It moves us beyond the search for a single, mythical "generalist" model that can conquer all market conditions.

Instead, we embrace the reality that the market is a composite of different environments. Our strategy, therefore, is to build not a single soldier, but a highly-trained **army of specialists**. Each hourly model is an expert, honed and optimized for the unique terrain and rhythm of its specific battlefield.

This approach—combining a robust, principled pipeline for model selection *within* a systematic, time-stratified exploration of market sessions—creates a holistic and powerful framework. It is a testament to the philosophy that success in the complex domain of financial markets is found not through a single, magic bullet, but through a disciplined, multi-layered strategy that respects the nuance and dynamism of time itself.

Chapter 18: Expanding the Informational Universe: A Framework for Multi-Asset Feature Integration

18.1 Introduction: Moving Beyond a Single-Pair Universe

Thus far, our modeling framework has been meticulously designed to extract predictive signals from the history of a single currency pair, EUR/USD. While powerful, this approach operates within a self-contained world. Financial markets, however, are not isolated ecosystems; they are deeply interconnected. The value of the U.S. dollar, global risk sentiment, and macroeconomic shifts create powerful currents that flow across all assets simultaneously.

A model that only sees EUR/USD has a myopic view of the market. To elevate its understanding, we can expand its informational universe by providing it with features derived from other, related assets. This could include other currency pairs (like GBP/USD or USD/JPY), commodity prices (like Oil or Gold), or even equity indices (like the S&P 500).

This chapter provides a conceptual and practical roadmap for integrating these external, cross-asset features into our existing four-stage modeling pipeline. We will explore the rationale for this approach and detail how our robust framework can systematically determine the true predictive value of this new information.

18.2 The Rationale for Cross-Asset Analysis

The logic for incorporating external data is rooted in the interconnectedness of the global financial system. Price movements in one asset are rarely independent events.

- **Shared Currency Drivers:** Many major pairs share a common currency, most notably the U.S. dollar. An event that strengthens or weakens the USD—such as a Federal Reserve policy announcement or a key U.S. employment report—will have a ripple effect across EUR/USD, GBP/USD, USD/JPY, and others. The price action in one pair can therefore act as a leading or confirming indicator for another.

- **Risk Sentiment and Capital Flows:** Certain assets are considered barometers of global risk appetite. For example, a rally in commodity-linked currencies like the Australian Dollar (AUD/USD) can signal a "risk-on" environment, while a flight to safe-haven assets like the Japanese Yen (USD/JPY) or Swiss Franc (USD/CHF) signals "risk-off" sentiment. These broad shifts in capital flows can be a powerful predictor of behavior in other pairs like EUR/USD.

- **Macroeconomic Spillover:** A significant economic event in one region (e.g., a policy shift by the European Central Bank) will primarily impact its own currency but will inevitably have spillover effects on its major trading partners. By providing the model with data from these related markets, we give it the potential to capture these complex, interconnected dynamics.

18.3 A Structured Framework for Integrating External Features

Integrating this new data does not require abandoning our robust pipeline. On the contrary, the pipeline's structured nature makes it perfectly suited to systematically evaluate and incorporate these new features. The process involves two key steps.

Step 1: The Expanded Data Preparation Phase

The first necessary change is to the initial data preparation script (the one that creates the 2.{...}_pandas.csv file). This script must be modified to:

1. **Load Multiple Datasets:** Instead of just loading EURUSD_60.csv, it would load data for all assets being considered (e.g., EURUSD_60.csv, GBPUSD_60.csv, USDJPY_60.csv).

2. **Align Timestamps:** It would merge these datasets based on their Date column, ensuring that each row represents the same moment in time across all assets.

3. **Calculate and Prefix Features:** It would then calculate technical indicators for each asset and save them with a clear prefix, for example: EURUSD_CCI, GBPUSD_CCI, USDJPY_ATR, etc.

The output would be a single, wide CSV file containing the Target variable for our primary pair (EUR/USD) alongside features from a whole universe of related assets.

Step 2: Letting the Pipeline "Speak" to the New Data

Once the unified dataset is created, the rest of the process leverages our existing four-stage pipeline with only a minor change. The new cross-asset features (e.g., USDJPY_ATR) are simply added to the all_potential_features list at the beginning of our main training script.

From there, our robust funnel takes over, letting the evidence guide the inclusion of these new features:

*   **In Stage 1 (compute_feature_selection):** The external features will compete on a level playing field with the native EUR/USD features. A feature like USDJPY_ATR will be tested for its statistical relevance (Mutual Information) to the **EUR/USD Target**. If it proves to be a strong, non-redundant predictor, it will be included in the "Base Feature Set." If not, it will be discarded.

- **In Stages 2, 3, and 4:** The subsequent model race, tuning, and backtesting will proceed as before, using the best features discovered in Stage 1, which may now be a sophisticated blend of indicators from multiple currency pairs.

This demonstrates the power of our framework. We do not need to guess if GBP/USD's momentum is relevant; we can introduce it as a candidate and trust our validated, data-driven process to determine its true predictive value.

18.4 Why This is Superior to Manual or Brute-Force Approaches

The integration of external features is an area where the superiority of our structured pipeline over manual selection or brute-force search becomes exceptionally clear.

- **Beyond Human Intuition:** A trader might have a hunch that the Japanese Yen's behavior influences the Euro. Our pipeline can **quantify** this intuition. compute_feature_selection will provide objective, statistical evidence of whether that relationship is strong enough to be included in the model, protecting us from narrative-based biases.

- **Avoiding a Combinatorial Nightmare:** Adding just 5 features from 3 other pairs would increase our initial feature pool by 15. For the brute-force "inverse selection" method, this would turn a computationally infeasible problem into an astronomically impossible one. Our pipeline handles this gracefully, as the cost of evaluating a few extra features in Stage 1 is trivial.

18.5 Conclusion: Building a Holistic, Data-Driven Worldview

By expanding our dataset to include features from other assets, we are fundamentally enriching our model's "worldview." We are allowing it to move beyond the narrow confines of a single instrument and begin to understand the broader, interconnected dynamics of the global financial system.

The true power of the framework we have built is its scalability and robustness. It provides a principled and efficient method for testing new hypotheses. The question, "Does the volatility of the Australian Dollar affect EUR/USD at 14:00?" is no longer a matter of opinion or endless manual analysis. It is a testable hypothesis that can be answered by adding the relevant feature to our pool and letting our validated, evidence-based pipeline deliver the verdict. This transforms model development from an exercise in guesswork into a true scientific process of discovery.

Chapter 19: From Theory to Practice: Implementing the Live Trading System in Python and MetaTrader 5

19.1 Introduction: Bridging the Gap Between Backtest and Reality

This chapter marks the final, crucial step in our journey: operationalizing the champion models produced by our robust development pipeline. This is where theory meets practice, and a validated strategy is transformed into an autonomous trading system. The goal is to build a Python application that can seamlessly interface with the MetaTrader 5 (MT5) platform to perform its duties: fetching real-time market data, calculating features, generating predictions from our saved model, and executing trades with disciplined risk management.

The paramount principle in this transition is **consistency**. The live environment's calculations, data handling, and feature engineering must perfectly mirror the conditions under which the model was trained and backtested. Any discrepancy can invalidate the model's edge. This chapter will walk through the architecture of our refactored live trading script, explaining how its modular, data-driven design ensures this consistency and creates a robust foundation for automated trading.

19.2 The Foundational Setup: Environment and Configuration

Before executing a single line of trading logic, we must establish a well-defined and stable foundation. This involves setting up the necessary libraries and, most importantly, centralizing the system's entire configuration.

a. Environment and Libraries

The script relies on a set of powerful Python libraries that serve as the backbone of its operations. A standard setup would include:

- **MetaTrader5**: The official API for all communication with the MT5 terminal.

- **pandas & numpy**: For high-performance data manipulation and numerical computation.

- **pandas-ta**: For calculating technical indicators consistently with our data preparation script.

- **scikit-learn, xgboost**: Required for loading and using the saved .pkl pipeline objects.

b. The Centralized Configuration Hub (STRATEGY_CONFIGS)

Instead of scattering dozens of hardcoded variables throughout the script, our system is driven by a single, clean, and easily modifiable data structure: the STRATEGY_CONFIGS list.

Example STRATEGY_CONFIGS from the refactored bot

```
1. STRATEGY_CONFIGS = [
2.    {
3.        "name": "Strategy 13:00 H1",
4.        "enabled": True,
5.        "model_path": "path/to/model_for_hour_13.pkl",
6.        "start_hour": 13,
7.        "start_minute": 0,
8.        "timeframe_str": "H1",
9.        "features": ['CCI', 'ADX_21', 'Inertia'],
10.        "tp_pips": 35,
11.        "sl_pips": 7,
12.        "magic_number": 13,
13.        "trade_type": "SELL",
14.        "probability_threshold": 0.53,
15.    },
16.    # ... Other strategy configurations ...
17. ]
18.
```

This design is a cornerstone of the system's robustness and scalability. All parameters for a given strategy—its name, the path to its dedicated model, its execution time, the features it requires, and its risk parameters—are defined in one place. Adding, removing, or modifying a strategy is as simple as editing this list, with no need to touch the core execution logic.

c. A Data-Driven Approach to Risk Parameters (TP and SL)

The tp_pips and sl_pips values within our configuration are not arbitrary numbers. A key part of the research process, following a successful backtest, is to determine appropriate risk parameters. While our pipeline focuses on entry signals, a complete strategy requires a thoughtful exit plan.

For our bar-by-bar prediction system, where the model predicts the direction of the next candle, TP and SL levels should be closely related to the **typical price movement within a single bar**. A robust method for determining these values involves:

1. **Analyzing Historical Volatility:** Using the backtest data, calculate the average range (High - Low) or the Average True Range (ATR) for the specific timeframe and session. This provides an empirical baseline for expected price movement.

2. **Backtesting Multiple Scenarios:** Re-run the backtest simulation multiple times with different TP/SL combinations that are proportional to the average volatility (e.g., TP = 60% of ATR, SL = 40% of ATR).

3. **Evaluating Performance Metrics:** For each scenario, analyze not just the final PnL, but also the **Win Rate**, **Profit Factor**, and **Maximum Drawdown**. The goal is to find a

combination that provides a favorable balance. A very tight SL might have a poor win rate but small losses, while a very wide TP might rarely get hit.

4. **Selecting the Optimal Balance:** The final values chosen for the configuration should be those that yielded a strong risk-adjusted return (e.g., a high Sharpe Ratio) during this sensitivity analysis.

19.3 The Architectural Blueprint: A Modular and Scalable Design

Our live trading script replaces a monolithic, repetitive structure with a clean, modular design that is easy to understand, debug, and extend.

- **The Main Loop: The System's Heartbeat:** The while True: loop acts as the central orchestrator. Its only job is to get the current server time and pass it to the processing functions in each cycle, ensuring the system is always monitoring the market.

- **The Configuration-Driven Core (process_strategy):** We do not have separate strategy_0() or strategy_13() functions. We have **one intelligent, generic function** that accepts a config dictionary as an argument. This single function contains all the logic for checking trade conditions, calculating features, making predictions, and placing trades. This eliminates code duplication and ensures all strategies are executed with the exact same logic.

- **Modular Helper Functions:** Common tasks are abstracted into their own functions (calculate_features, place_trade, check_order_placed). This adheres to the single-responsibility principle, making the code cleaner and more readable.

19.4 An Example of Strategy Specialization: The "Buy-Only" Mandate

A powerful feature of our session-based modeling approach is the ability to create highly specialized strategies. The decision to configure a model to *only* take BUY trades or *only* take SELL trades should be a direct, data-driven conclusion from the backtesting stage.

Imagine that after running our training pipeline for the 13:00 hour, the backtest_model function produces the following results:

- **Overall PnL:** +\$541

- **BUY Opportunities PnL:** -\$1,200 (The model consistently loses money when it tries to predict upward movements)

- **SELL Opportunities PnL:** +\$1,741 (The model is highly profitable when predicting downward movements)

108

The evidence is clear. For this specific time of day, our champion model has a significant, exploitable edge in predicting SELL opportunities but is ineffective at predicting BUYs. The logical, data-driven action is to intervene at the configuration level. In our STRATEGY_CONFIGS, we would set the trade_type for this strategy to "SELL" and potentially increase its probability_threshold to be even more selective.

This is not a preconceived bias. It is a strategic optimization based on the robust evidence generated by our backtesting process, allowing us to deploy only the parts of our model's "knowledge" that have proven to be profitable.

19.5 The Lifecycle of a Live Model: The Importance of Retraining

No model, no matter how robustly validated, will remain optimal forever. Markets evolve, and a model's predictive edge, known as "alpha," will naturally decay over time. Therefore, a professional trading system must include a process for periodic retraining.

This involves:

1. **Continuous Data Collection:** Regularly appending new market data to our historical dataset.

2. **Scheduled Re-validation:** Establishing a schedule (e.g., quarterly or semi-annually) to re-run the entire four-stage training pipeline on the updated dataset.

3. **Deploying the New Champion:** If the pipeline produces a new champion model that demonstrates superior performance on the most recent data, it replaces the old model in the live trading environment.

This disciplined cycle of **Deploy -> Monitor -> Retrain -> Redeploy** ensures the system adapts to long-term changes in market structure and prevents the slow decay that dooms static trading strategies.

19.6 Conclusion: The Trader as a System Architect

This chapter has demonstrated how to translate a validated model into a live, operational trading system. The resulting Python application is not merely a script that executes trades; it is a reflection of our entire robust methodology.

In this paradigm, the role of the quantitative trader evolves. The focus shifts from making individual buy/sell decisions to a higher level of strategic oversight. The trader becomes the **architect and manager of a decision-making ecosystem,** responsible for designing the data pipeline, governing the experimental framework, monitoring live performance, and directing the crucial cycle of retraining and adaptation. This framework provides the tools to manage that ecosystem with discipline, evidence, and confidence.

Chapter 20: From Theory to Practice: Implementing the Live Trading System

20.1 Introduction: Bridging the Gap Between Backtest and Reality

This chapter marks the culmination of our entire modeling journey: the operationalization of a validated trading strategy. We transition from the historical, analytical environment of backtesting to the dynamic, real-time world of live execution. The objective is to construct a robust Python application that serves as the bridge, connecting the intelligence of our trained machine learning models to the execution capabilities of the MetaTrader 5 (MT5) platform.

The paramount principle governing this transition is **consistency**. The methods used to calculate features, handle data, and generate predictions in the live environment must be a perfect mirror of the processes used during training and backtesting. Any discrepancy, no matter how small, can invalidate the statistical edge we have worked so meticulously to discover.

This chapter will dissect the architectural blueprint of our refactored live trading script. We will explore how its modular, object-oriented design not only ensures this critical consistency but also creates a system that is scalable, maintainable, and resilient.

20.2 The Architectural Philosophy: A Modular, Configuration-Driven Design

A trading bot can be architected as a single, monolithic script with hardcoded logic. This approach, however, is brittle, difficult to debug, and nearly impossible to scale. Our framework deliberately rejects this in favor of a modern software design principle: the **separation of configuration from logic**.

- **Configuration (The "What"):** We define *what* each strategy is—its parameters, its model, the features it needs—in a centralized, easy-to-edit data structure.

- **Logic (The "How"):** We create a generic, reusable engine that contains the logic for *how* to execute a strategy, regardless of its specific parameters.

This design transforms our trading bot from a rigid script into a flexible, dynamic system.

20.3 Core Components of the Live Trading Framework

Our live trading application is built upon several key components that work in concert.

a) The Centralized Configuration Hub (STRATEGY_CONFIGS)

This list of dictionaries is the control panel for the entire system. It is the single source of truth that defines every strategy the bot can execute.

```
1. # The STRATEGY_CONFIGS list from the live trading script
2. STRATEGY_CONFIGS = [
3.    {
4.       "name": "Strategy 13:00 H1",
5.       "enabled": True,  # Allows easy activation/deactivation
6.       "model_path": "path/to/model_for_hour_13.pkl",
7.       "start_hour": 13,
8.       "start_minute": 0,
9.       "timeframe_str": "H1",
10.      "features": ['CCI', 'ADX_21', 'Inertia'],
11.      "tp_pips": 35,
12.      "sl_pips": 7,
13.      "magic_number": 13001,
14.      "trade_type": "SELL",  # Can be 'BUY', 'SELL', or 'BOTH'
15.      "probability_threshold": 0.55,
16.   },
17.   # ... Other strategy configurations can be added here ...
18. ]
19.
```

This structure makes the system incredibly scalable and maintainable. To add a new trading strategy, one simply adds a new dictionary to this list. To adjust the Take Profit for an existing strategy, only a single value needs to be changed. This eliminates the need to hunt through hundreds of lines of code, reducing the risk of error. The enabled key is particularly useful, allowing a strategy to be turned on or off without deleting its configuration.

b) The Strategy Class: The Object-Oriented Engine

To avoid the pitfalls of repetitive code and complex global state management, our framework uses an object-oriented approach. The Strategy class serves as a "blueprint" for any trading strategy we wish to implement.

- **Initialization (__init__)**: When the script starts, it creates a separate Strategy object for each configuration in the STRATEGY_CONFIGS list. The __init__ method acts as a constructor, taking a config dictionary and assigning its values to the object's attributes (like self.name, self.start_hour, etc.). Crucially, it also manages the object's internal state, such as self.prediction_made_today, ensuring that the state of one strategy does not interfere with another.

- **Model Loading (_load_pipeline)**: For efficiency, each Strategy object loads its corresponding .pkl model file *once* during initialization. This private method handles opening the file and loading the complete Scikit-learn Pipeline object, which includes both the data scaler and the trained classifier. Robust error handling ensures that if a model file is missing, the failure is logged, and the strategy is safely disabled.

112

- **Feature Calculation (_calculate_features)**: This method is responsible for fetching the latest market data from MT5 and calculating the technical indicators. It is designed for maximum consistency:

    o It dynamically inspects the strategy's self.required_features list.

    o It calculates *only* the indicators present in that list, using the exact same pandas_ta library and parameters as our data preparation script.

    o It returns the features for the most recently closed candle (.iloc[-2:-1]), which is a critical step to avoid lookahead bias by ensuring the model only uses fully formed, historical information to make its prediction.

- **Execution Logic (execute)**: This is the main method for each strategy object, called on every tick by the main loop. It contains the complete decision-making logic:

0. It first checks internal state variables, like resetting self.prediction_made_today at the start of a new day.

1. It verifies if the current server time matches the strategy's start_hour and start_minute.

2. It checks for locks, ensuring it doesn't trade if it has already made a prediction today or if another strategy has already opened a trade in the current session.

3. If all conditions are met, it calls self._calculate_features() to get the latest indicator values.

4. It feeds these features into its loaded pipeline, calling both .predict() to get the binary outcome (0 or 1) and .predict_proba() to get the model's confidence score.

5. Finally, it applies the trade logic, checking if the prediction matches the configured trade_type and if the model's confidence (probability) exceeds the probability_threshold. If all checks pass, it initiates a trade and signals back to the main loop that a trade has been placed.

c) Helper Functions for MT5 Interaction

Common tasks that involve communicating with the MT5 server are abstracted into modular helper functions:

- **initialize_mt5**: Establishes and verifies the connection to the MT5 terminal, with built-in retries and error reporting.

- **send_telegram_message**: Provides crucial oversight by sending real-time alerts for trade entries, failures, and critical errors.

- **check_order_placed**: Uses a strategy's unique magic_number to query MT5 and determine if that specific strategy already has an open position, preventing duplicate trades.

- **place_trade**: This function constructs the final order request dictionary with all necessary parameters (symbol, volume, type, price, sl, tp, magic, etc.) and sends it to the server using mt.order_send(). It includes a vital **spread protector** to abort the trade if market conditions are unfavorable, and it performs the correct calculation for sl and tp levels based on the instrument's point size.

20.4 The Main Execution Loop: An Elegant Orchestrator

The if __name__ == "__main__": block serves as the conductor of our system. Its design is clean and purposeful:

1. **Initialization:** It connects to MT5 and then instantiates all the Strategy objects based on the STRATEGY_CONFIGS list.

2. **Session Management:** It initializes a single boolean variable, order_traded_this_session. This acts as a global lock, ensuring that after one strategy successfully places a trade, no other strategies will attempt to open a new trade for the remainder of the trading day. This prevents the bot from over-trading. This lock is reset once per day at server midnight.

3. **The Infinite Loop:** The while True: loop is the heartbeat of the bot. In every iteration, it gets the current server time and loops through its list of instantiated Strategy objects, calling the execute() method on each one. If any strategy reports that it has placed a trade, the order_traded_this_session lock is activated, and the loop breaks for that tick. The time.sleep(1) call ensures the loop runs at a manageable pace, preventing CPU overload and excessive API calls.

20.5 Conclusion: The Trader as a Systems Architect

This chapter has detailed the transformation of a validated model into a live, operational trading system. The resulting Python application, built on principles of modularity and configuration-driven logic, is not merely a script that executes trades; it is a robust and scalable framework for automated strategy deployment.

In this paradigm, the role of the quantitative trader evolves. The focus shifts from the tactical execution of individual trades to the strategic oversight of a complex decision-making ecosystem. The modern quant trader is a **systems architect**, responsible for designing the data pipelines, governing the experimental framework, monitoring live performance, and directing the crucial cycle of adaptation and retraining. This robust codebase provides the essential tools to manage that ecosystem with the discipline, evidence, and confidence required to succeed in today's financial markets.

```python
1. # -*- coding: utf-8 -*-
2. """
3. LIVE TRADING BOT FOR METATRADER 5
4.
5. This script implements a multi-strategy algorithmic trading system that
6. interfaces with the MetaTrader 5 platform.
7.
8. Architecture:
9. - It uses a configuration-driven approach where all strategies are defined in a
10.    central `STRATEGY_CONFIGS` list.
11. - An object-oriented design with a `Strategy` class encapsulates the logic
12.    and state for each individual trading strategy.
13. - It operates in a continuous loop, monitoring market data, and executing
14.    trades based on predictions from pre-trained machine learning models.
15. - Includes utilities for trade management, risk control (spread protection),
16.    and real-time notifications via Telegram.
17. """
18.
19. import os
20. import pickle
21. import datetime
22. import time
23. import traceback
24. import requests
25. import json
26. import warnings
27.
28. import MetaTrader5 as mt
29. import pandas as pd
30. import pandas_ta as ta
31.
32. # --- 1. GENERAL CONFIGURATION ---
33. warnings.filterwarnings("ignore")
34.
35. # --- Telegram Configuration ---
36. BOT_TOKEN = "YOUR_TELEGRAM_BOT_TOKEN" # <--- IMPORTANT: REPLACE WITH YOUR TOKEN
37. CHAT_ID = "YOUR_TELEGRAM_CHAT_ID"   # <--- IMPORTANT: REPLACE WITH YOUR CHAT ID
38.
39. # --- Trading Parameters ---
40. SYMBOL = "EURUSD"
41. LOTS = 0.01  # Use float for volume
42. COMMENT = "Artilect-AI v2.0"
43. SPREAD_PROTECTOR_PIPS = 1.5  # Do not trade if spread is wider than this in pips
44.
45. # --- Timeframe Mapping (from string to MT5 constant) ---
46. TIMEFRAME_MAP = {
47.    "M15": mt.TIMEFRAME_M15,
48.    "M30": mt.TIMEFRAME_M30,
49.    "H1": mt.TIMEFRAME_H1,
50. }
51.
52. # --- 2. STRATEGY CONFIGURATION HUB ---
53. # This is the control panel for all strategies.
54. # To add, remove, or modify a strategy, simply edit its dictionary here.
55. STRATEGY_CONFIGS = [
56.    {
57.        "name": "Strategy 13:00 H1",
58.        "enabled": True,  # Allows easy activation/deactivation
59.        "model_path":
"EURUSD_hour13_minute0_model_results/profit_541.00_EURUSD_XGBoost_f1w_0.5888_TUNED_features_CCI_ADX21_Inertia_t
f60_hour13_minute0.pkl",
```

115

```
60.        "start_hour": 13,
61.        "start_minute": 0,
62.        "timeframe_str": "H1",
63.        "features": ['CCI', 'ADX_21', 'Inertia'],
64.        "tp_pips": 35,
65.        "sl_pips": 7,
66.        "magic_number": 13001,
67.        "trade_type": "SELL",  # Can be 'BUY', 'SELL', or 'BOTH'
68.        "probability_threshold": 0.55,
69.    },
70.    {
71.        "name": "Strategy 01:00 M30",
72.        "enabled": True,
73.        "model_path":
"EURUSD_hour1_minute0_model_results/profit_8174.00_EURUSD_RadiusNeighbors_f1w_0.7106_TUNED_features_CCI_Inertia_tf
30_hour1_minute0.pkl",
74.        "start_hour": 1,
75.        "start_minute": 0,
76.        "timeframe_str": "M30",
77.        "features": ['CCI', 'Inertia'],
78.        "tp_pips": 6,
79.        "sl_pips": 19,
80.        "magic_number": 1001,
81.        "trade_type": "SELL",
82.        "probability_threshold": 0.70,
83.    },
84.    {
85.        "name": "Strategy 17:15 M15",
86.        "enabled": True,
87.        "model_path":
"EURUSD_hour17_minute15_model_results/profit_3274.00_EURUSD_AdaBoost_f1w_0.5957_TUNED_features_CCI_VHF_tf15_hou
r17_minute15.pkl",
88.        "start_hour": 17,
89.        "start_minute": 15,
90.        "timeframe_str": "M15",
91.        "features": ['CCI', 'VHF'],
92.        "tp_pips": 19,
93.        "sl_pips": 6,
94.        "magic_number": 17151,
95.        "trade_type": "SELL",
96.        "probability_threshold": 0.55,
97.    },
98. ]
99.
100.
101. # --- 3. THE STRATEGY CLASS ---
102. class Strategy:
103.     """Encapsulates the logic and state for a single trading strategy."""
104.     def __init__(self, config):
105.         # Assign static configuration
106.         self.name = config["name"]
107.         self.enabled = config.get("enabled", True)
108.         self.model_path = config["model_path"]
109.         self.start_hour = config["start_hour"]
110.         self.start_minute = config["start_minute"]
111.         self.timeframe = TIMEFRAME_MAP[config["timeframe_str"]]
112.         self.required_features = config["features"]
113.         self.tp_pips = config["tp_pips"]
114.         self.sl_pips = config["sl_pips"]
115.         self.magic_number = config["magic_number"]
116.         self.trade_type = config["trade_type"]
117.         self.probability_threshold = config.get("probability_threshold", 0.51)
118.
119.         # Internal state for this strategy instance
120.         self.pipeline = self._load_pipeline()
121.         self.prediction_made_today = False
```

```python
122.        self.last_checked_day = -1
123.
124.    def _load_pipeline(self):
125.        """Loads the pickled model pipeline once at initialization."""
126.        if not os.path.exists(self.model_path):
127.            print(f"ERROR: [{self.name}] Model file not found: {self.model_path}")
128.            return None
129.        try:
130.            with open(self.model_path, 'rb') as f:
131.                print(f"[{self.name}] Model loaded successfully from: {self.model_path}")
132.                return pickle.load(f)
133.        except Exception as e:
134.            print(f"ERROR: [{self.name}] Failed to load model: {e}")
135.            send_telegram_message(f"🚨 CRITICAL ERROR: Could not load model for {self.name}")
136.            return None
137.
138.    def _calculate_features(self, server_time):
139.        """Fetches data and calculates the specific indicators required by this strategy."""
140.        df = pd.DataFrame(mt.copy_rates_from(SYMBOL, self.timeframe, server_time, 200))
141.        if df.empty:
142.            return None
143.        df["time"] = pd.to_datetime(df["time"], unit="s")
144.
145.        # Dynamically calculate only the required features
146.        all_features = pd.DataFrame(index=df.index)
147.        if 'CCI' in self.required_features: all_features['CCI'] = ta.cci(df["high"], df["low"], df["close"], length=14)
148.        if 'ADX_21' in self.required_features: all_features['ADX_21'] = ta.adx(df["high"], df["low"], df["close"], length=21).iloc[:, 0]
149.        if 'Inertia' in self.required_features: all_features['Inertia'] = ta.inertia(df["close"], df["high"], df["low"], length=21)
150.        if 'VHF' in self.required_features: all_features['VHF'] = ta.vhf(df["close"], length=21)
151.        if 'ATR' in self.required_features: all_features['ATR'] = ta.atr(df['high'], df['low'], df['close'], length=21)
152.        if 'RSI' in self.required_features: all_features['RSI'] = ta.rsi(df["close"], length=14)
153.        # Add other indicators as needed...
154.
155.        # Return the last row (most recent closed candle) with the required features
156.        return all_features[self.required_features].iloc[-2:-1]
157.
158.    def execute(self, server_time, session_lock):
159.        """Main execution logic for this strategy, called on every tick."""
160.        if not self.enabled or not self.pipeline:
161.            return False  # Strategy is disabled or model failed to load
162.
163.        # Reset the "once-per-day" trigger at midnight
164.        if server_time.day != self.last_checked_day:
165.            self.prediction_made_today = False
166.            self.last_checked_day = server_time.day
167.
168.        # Check if it's time to trade
169.        is_trade_time = (server_time.hour == self.start_hour and server_time.minute == self.start_minute)
170.
171.        # Entry conditions
172.        if is_trade_time and not self.prediction_made_today and not check_order_placed(self.magic_number) and not session_lock:
173.            self.prediction_made_today = True  # Prevent re-entry today
174.
175.            print(f"\n--- [{self.name}] Initiating Trading Period ---")
176.
177.            features_df = self._calculate_features(server_time)
178.            if features_df is None or features_df.isnull().values.any():
179.                print(f"[{self.name}] Could not calculate features or found NaNs. Skipping trade.")
180.                return False
181.
182.            # Make prediction
183.            prediction = self.pipeline.predict(features_df)[0]
184.            probabilities = self.pipeline.predict_proba(features_df)[0]
185.            prob_sell, prob_buy = round(probabilities[0], 2), round(probabilities[1], 2)
186.
187.            print(f"[{self.name}] Features: \n{features_df.to_string(index=False)}")
```

```python
188.        print(f"[{self.name}] Prediction: {prediction} (0=SELL, 1=BUY) | Probabilities: [SELL={prob_sell}, BUY={prob_buy}]")
189.        send_telegram_message(f"📈 Signal for [{self.name}]\nPred: {prediction}, P(SELL): {prob_sell}, P(BUY): {prob_buy}")
190.
191.        # Decision logic
192.        if (self.trade_type == "BUY" or self.trade_type == "BOTH") and prediction == 1 and prob_buy >=
self.probability_threshold:
193.            print(f"[{self.name}] BUY signal confirmed.")
194.            place_trade(self, mt.ORDER_TYPE_BUY)
195.            return True  # Signal that a trade was placed
196.        elif (self.trade_type == "SELL" or self.trade_type == "BOTH") and prediction == 0 and prob_sell >=
self.probability_threshold:
197.            print(f"[{self.name}] SELL signal confirmed.")
198.            place_trade(self, mt.ORDER_TYPE_SELL)
199.            return True  # Signal that a trade was placed
200.        else:
201.            print(f"[{self.name}] Signal did not meet conditions. No trade placed.")
202.
203.        return False  # No trade was placed in this cycle
204.
205.
206. # --- 4. HELPER FUNCTIONS FOR MT5 INTERACTION ---
207.
208. def initialize_mt5():
209.     """Establishes and checks the connection to MetaTrader 5."""
210.     if not mt.initialize():
211.         print("Initialize() failed, retrying...")
212.         time.sleep(5)
213.         if not mt.initialize():
214.             print("Could not connect to MetaTrader 5 terminal.")
215.             send_telegram_message("🔴 FATAL ERROR: Could not connect to MT5 terminal.")
216.             return False
217.     print("MetaTrader 5 connection successful.")
218.     return True
219.
220. def send_telegram_message(message):
221.     """Sends a message to a pre-defined Telegram chat."""
222.     if not BOT_TOKEN or not CHAT_ID: return
223.     try:
224.         url = f"https://api.telegram.org/bot{BOT_TOKEN}/sendMessage"
225.         data = {"chat_id": CHAT_ID, "text": message}
226.         requests.post(url, data=data, timeout=10)
227.     except Exception as e:
228.         print(f"Error sending Telegram message: {e}")
229.
230. def check_order_placed(magic_number):
231.     """Checks if a trade with a specific magic number is already open."""
232.     positions = mt.positions_get(symbol=SYMBOL)
233.     if positions:
234.         for pos in positions:
235.             if pos.magic == magic_number:
236.                 return True
237.     return False
238.
239. def place_trade(strategy, order_type):
240.     """Constructs and sends a trade request to the MT5 server."""
241.     tick = mt.symbol_info_tick(SYMBOL)
242.     if not tick:
243.         print(f"[{strategy.name}] Could not get tick data. Trade aborted.")
244.         return
245.
246.     spread_pips = round((tick.ask - tick.bid) / (mt.symbol_info(SYMBOL).point * 10))
247.     if spread_pips > SPREAD_PROTECTOR_PIPS:
248.         msg = f"[{strategy.name}] Spread too high ({spread_pips} pips). Trade aborted."
249.         print(msg)
250.         send_telegram_message(f"⚠️ {msg}")
```

```python
251.       return
252.
253.    price = tick.ask if order_type == mt.ORDER_TYPE_BUY else tick.bid
254.    point = mt.symbol_info(SYMBOL).point
255.
256.    sl = price - strategy.sl_pips * 10 * point if order_type == mt.ORDER_TYPE_BUY else price + strategy.sl_pips * 10 * point
257.    tp = price + strategy.tp_pips * 10 * point if order_type == mt.ORDER_TYPE_BUY else price - strategy.tp_pips * 10 * point
258.
259.    request = {
260.        "action": mt.TRADE_ACTION_DEAL,
261.        "symbol": SYMBOL,
262.        "volume": LOTS,
263.        "type": order_type,
264.        "price": price,
265.        "sl": round(sl, 5),
266.        "tp": round(tp, 5),
267.        "magic": strategy.magic_number,
268.        "comment": f"{COMMENT} [{strategy.name}]",
269.        "type_time": mt.ORDER_TIME_GTC,
270.        "type_filling": mt.ORDER_FILLING_IOC,
271.    }
272.
273.    result = mt.order_send(request)
274.
275.    print("--- Trade Execution Result ---")
276.    if result.retcode == mt.TRADE_RETCODE_DONE:
277.        msg = f"✅ TRADE OPENED: [{strategy.name}]\nType: {'BUY' if order_type == mt.ORDER_TYPE_BUY else 'SELL'} @ {price}"
278.        print(msg)
279.        send_telegram_message(msg)
280.    else:
281.        msg = f"❌ TRADE FAILED: [{strategy.name}]\nCode: {result.retcode} - {result.comment}"
282.        print(msg)
283.        send_telegram_message(msg)
284.    print("--------------------------")
285.
286.
287. # --- 5. MAIN EXECUTION BLOCK ---
288. def main():
289.    """Main function to initialize and run the trading bot."""
290.    if not initialize_mt5():
291.        return
292.
293.    print("--- Artilect AI Trading Bot Initializing ---")
294.    print(f"Monitoring Symbol: {SYMBOL}, Lot Size: {LOTS}")
295.
296.    # Create an instance of each enabled strategy
297.    strategies = [Strategy(config) for config in STRATEGY_CONFIGS if config.get("enabled", True)]
298.    print(f"Loaded and enabled {len(strategies)} strategies.")
299.    send_telegram_message(f"🤖 Bot Initialized. {len(strategies)} strategies active.")
300.
301.    # A global lock to ensure only one trade is opened per session/day
302.    order_traded_this_session = False
303.
304.    while True:
305.        try:
306.            tick = mt.symbol_info_tick(SYMBOL)
307.            if not tick:
308.                time.sleep(2)  # Wait if market data is unavailable
309.                continue
310.
311.            server_time = pd.to_datetime(tick.time, unit='s')
312.
313.            # Reset the session lock at midnight server time
314.            if server_time.hour == 0 and server_time.minute < 2:
```

```
315.            if order_traded_this_session:
316.                print(f"Server midnight reached. Unlocking session for new trades.")
317.                send_telegram_message("🔓 Daily session lock has been reset.")
318.                order_traded_this_session = False
319.
320.            # Iterate through strategies and execute their logic
321.            for strategy in strategies:
322.                trade_was_placed = strategy.execute(server_time, order_traded_this_session)
323.                if trade_was_placed:
324.                    order_traded_this_session = True
325.                    print(f"[{strategy.name}] placed a trade. Session is now locked.")
326.                    send_telegram_message(f"🔒 Session locked by [{strategy.name}]. No more new trades today.")
327.                    break  # Stop checking other strategies for this tick
328.
329.            time.sleep(1)  # Main loop heartbeat
330.
331.        except Exception as e:
332.            print(f"CRITICAL ERROR in main loop: {e}")
333.            traceback.print_exc()
334.            send_telegram_message(f"🔥 CRITICAL ERROR in main loop: {e}")
335.            time.sleep(60) # Wait longer after a critical error
336.
337. if __name__ == "__main__":
338.    main()
339.
```

Chapter 21: A Universal Framework: Adapting the System to New Platforms and Instruments

21.1 Introduction: The Power of a Modular and Agnostic Core

Throughout this book, we have meticulously constructed a robust pipeline for developing and deploying a trading model for the EUR/USD pair on the MetaTrader 5 platform. However, the true power of this framework lies not in its application to a single instrument, but in its inherent **modularity and portability**. The core intellectual property—our four-stage validation methodology and the resulting champion models—is fundamentally independent of any single trading platform or asset class.

A well-architected system separates its core logic from its implementation details. Our pipeline is designed precisely this way. This chapter provides a practical blueprint for adapting this core logic to new environments. We will explore how to apply our system to different instruments, such as stocks, commodities, or cryptocurrencies, and how to migrate the execution logic to other popular trading platforms, demonstrating the universal applicability of a principled, data-driven approach.

21.2 The Blueprint for Adaptation: A Three-Part Process

Adapting our system to a new instrument or platform is not an ad-hoc process but a structured one that mirrors the separation of concerns in our codebase. The adaptation involves three distinct layers: the Data Layer, the Logic Layer, and the Execution Layer.

- **Part 1: The Data Abstraction Layer (Modifying the Data Preparation Script)** The first step is always to adapt the data ingestion process. Our data_preparation.py script would be modified to pull historical data for the new instrument (e.g., Apple stock - AAPL, or Bitcoin - BTC/USD) from its specific source (e.g., a financial data provider like Yahoo Finance, or a cryptocurrency exchange API). The crucial requirement is that the script must process this raw data and save it in our **standardized CSV format**, with the essential Date, Open, High, Low, and Close columns. As long as the output format is consistent, the next stage of the pipeline can function seamlessly.

- **Part 2: The Logic Layer (Re-running the Training Pipeline)** This is where the power of our generic framework becomes evident. Once the new, standardized data file is prepared (e.g., 2.AAPL_60_pandas.csv), our existing training and validation script can be used **with almost no modification**. We simply change the pair and tf variables to point to the new data file. The entire four-stage pipeline will then execute automatically, discovering the best features, model architecture, and hyperparameters specifically for that new instrument. It will produce a new champion model (e.g., AAPL_RandomForest_..._TUNED.pkl) that is expertly tailored to the unique dynamics of that asset.

- **Part 3: The Execution Abstraction Layer (Modifying the Live Trading Bot)** This is where platform-specific changes are required. The beauty of our bot's modular design is that we only need to rewrite the small number of helper functions that directly communicate with the trading API. The core Strategy class and the main while loop logic remain almost entirely unchanged.

  - initialize_mt5() would be replaced with initialize_binance().

  - place_trade() would be rewritten to use the new platform's order submission syntax.

  - check_order_placed() would query the new platform's API for open positions.

By abstracting the execution details, we can "plug in" different platforms without having to re-engineer the entire trading logic.

21.3 Case Study 1: Adapting to a New Instrument (Gold - XAU/USD) on the Same Platform

Let's say we want to trade Gold on MT5. The process would be:

1. **Data Layer:** Modify the data preparation script to download historical XAU/USD data from MT5, calculate all technical indicators, and save the result as 2.XAUUSD_60_pandas.csv.

2. **Logic Layer:** Run our main training script, setting pair = "XAUUSD". The pipeline will execute its four stages. We might discover that for Gold, volatility features like ATR are far more important than they were for EUR/USD. The process will conclude by saving a new champion model, e.g., XAUUSD_GradientBoosting_..._TUNED.pkl.

3. **Execution Layer:** In our existing live trading bot, we simply add a new strategy dictionary to the STRATEGY_CONFIGS list, setting name = "Gold Strategy", model_path to the new Gold model file, and ensuring the magic_number is unique.

Because we are on the same platform, no changes to the execution functions are needed. The system is now trading both EUR/USD and Gold, each with its own specialized model.

21.4 Case Study 2: Adapting to a New Platform (Binance for Cryptocurrencies)

122

Let's say we want to trade BTC/USDT on Binance.

1. **Data Layer:** Write a new data preparation script using the python-binance library to fetch historical BTC/USDT k-line data from Binance. Process it and save it in our standard 2.BTCUSDT_60_pandas.csv format.

2. **Logic Layer:** Run the training script with pair = "BTCUSDT". The pipeline will analyze Bitcoin's unique, high-volatility dynamics and produce a champion model specifically trained to understand them.

3. **Execution Layer:** This requires the most work, but it is highly contained. We would create a new bot_binance.py file.

   o The Strategy class and the main while loop can be copied over directly.

   o We would rewrite the helper functions: initialize_binance() would handle API key authentication. place_trade() would use client.create_order() from the Binance API. check_order_placed() would query client.get_open_orders().

   o Update the STRATEGY_CONFIGS list to point to our new Bitcoin model.

Once this one-time adaptation of the execution functions is complete, we have a fully functional cryptocurrency trading bot that leverages the same robust core logic as our forex bot.

21.5 Conclusion: The Value of a Universal Architecture

The effort invested in building a clean, modular, and configuration-driven architecture pays enormous dividends in portability and scalability. The core of our system—the principled, data-driven methodology for discovering and validating profitable strategies—is a reusable intellectual asset.

By abstracting the data sources and execution venues into swappable components, we have created a truly universal framework for quantitative research and deployment. It allows us to ask sophisticated questions like, "How would this strategy perform on Japanese equities?" or "Can we adapt this model to trade oil futures?" and provides a clear, efficient path to finding the answers. This elevates our work from building a single trading bot to creating a powerful, adaptable engine for strategy innovation across any market or platform we choose to explore.

Chapter 22: Final Thoughts and Conclusion – The Trader's Journey

As we approach the conclusion of this book, it is vital to pause and reflect on the remarkable journey we have undertaken. We began with a fundamental challenge: how to navigate the complex, noisy, and ever-changing financial markets with a data-driven strategy that is both powerful and reliable. We have moved from basic concepts to the construction of a complete, end-to-end machine learning pipeline, designed not just to find signals, but to do so with statistical rigor and intellectual honesty.

This final chapter revisits the core philosophy that has guided our process, emphasizing the critical balance between exploration and discipline, and outlining a path forward for those who wish to continue evolving as traders in a world of rapid technological advancement.

The Core Philosophy: A Principled, Data-Driven Approach

A foundational principle of this book has been the development of a trading methodology guided by evidence, not by preconceived biases or unconstrained searching. In a field where many rely on fixed strategies or a favorite indicator, our approach is different: it embraces uncertainty by trusting a **robust process** to uncover a statistical edge.

This is a critical distinction. A naïve interpretation of "letting the data speak" can lead to a chaotic, brute-force search that overfits to historical noise. Our methodology is the antithesis of this. It is a structured dialogue with the data, where agnosticism is applied strategically:

- We are **agnostic about outcomes**, making no prior assumptions about which model architecture or feature set will prove most effective for a given market regime.

- We are **dogmatic about process**, adhering to a strict, four-stage funnel of validation that ensures the conclusions we draw are statistically sound and robust.

Adaptability in our framework is not achieved through a single model that changes itself in real-time. It is achieved through a resilient **"model factory"**—our pipeline—that allows us to build new, better-adapted models as market conditions evolve. The edge lies not in a single secret formula, but in the discipline of the system.

The Power of Machine Learning as a Tool

The integration of machine learning has been central to our journey. As we have demonstrated, algorithms like XGBoost and RandomForest, when properly implemented within a sound framework, can uncover complex, non-linear patterns that would be impossible for a human to detect manually. They can process and synthesize information from multiple indicators simultaneously, providing a probabilistic edge.

However, we must reinforce a crucial lesson: machine learning is a powerful **tool**, not a panacea. Its effectiveness is entirely dependent on the quality of the data it is fed and the integrity of the process used to train and validate it. The trader who understands that their role is to be the architect of this process—to ensure the data is clean, the features are relevant, the validation is honest, and the risks are managed—is the one who will unlock the true potential of this technology.

Embracing Continuous Learning: Markets Evolve, and So Must We

In the world of trading, stagnation is the precursor to failure. A key theme of this book has been the necessity of continuous learning and adaptation.

- **Regular Model Retraining:** Market regimes shift. The patterns of a post-pandemic recovery are not the same as those of a high-inflation environment. Our system is designed around this reality. "Retraining" means periodically re-running the entire **four-stage validation pipeline** on new and relevant data. This disciplined cycle of deploying a champion model, monitoring its performance, and regenerating a new champion when evidence suggests the market has changed is the key to long-term survival and success.

- **Learning from Every Trade:** Beyond the model, the trader must also evolve. Every backtest and every live trade—whether a win or a loss—is a data point. Analyzing why a model succeeded in one environment and failed in another deepens our understanding and informs the next iteration of our research. This mindset of intellectual curiosity and resilience is the hallmark of a successful quantitative trader.

Risk Management: The Unwavering Heart of Success

No chapter on trading would be complete without a final, emphatic statement on the primacy of risk management. No model is infallible. Losses are not just possible; they are a statistical certainty. A strategy's success is ultimately defined not by its winning trades, but by its ability to survive its losing ones.

Disciplined risk management—through carefully determined **stop-losses**, appropriate **position sizing**, and a deep understanding of the model's historical **drawdowns**—is the heart of any long-term trading operation. Our live trading framework integrates these components, but the wisdom to respect them lies with the system's human architect.

The Trader's Evolving Role

The journey through this book has been about more than just code; it has been about a transformation in the role of the trader. The framework we have built elevates the trader from a "signal-follower" to a **"systems architect."**

The modern quantitative trader's edge is found not in a faster trigger finger or a secret indicator, but in the ability to design, manage, and continuously improve a complex decision-making ecosystem. Their responsibilities are to:

1. Curate high-quality data.

2. Engineer insightful features.

3. Govern a robust validation framework.

4. Critically interpret the results.

5. Manage risk with unwavering discipline.

6. Know when the evidence demands that the system must evolve.

Final Words

The methodology presented in this book is a framework for thought and a blueprint for action. It is not a static, "get rich quick" system, but a dynamic process for engaging with the markets in an intelligent, data-driven, and disciplined manner.

By embracing a principled approach, you free yourself from the constraints of rigid thinking and the perils of chasing random noise. You empower yourself to adapt, learn, and evolve alongside the markets, armed with a process designed to separate true signal from the endless chaos.

Thank you for undertaking this journey. May your path forward be one of continuous learning, rigorous analysis, and lasting success. Good luck.

Appendix: A Practical Toolkit and Reference Guide

The Appendix serves as a comprehensive reference, offering additional details, tools, and resources to enhance your understanding and implementation of the concepts covered in this book. Here, you'll find the specific Python libraries that power our framework, detailed steps for setting up MetaTrader 5 (MT5), an overview of the key technical indicators used as feature candidates, and a concise summary of our unique machine learning workflow. This section is designed to support your ongoing development, providing practical resources that will enable you to expand and refine the strategies presented.

A.1 Python Libraries Used

Python is the engine of our entire trading system, providing powerful libraries for data processing, machine learning, and platform integration. Below are the key libraries used throughout this book:

- **MetaTrader5**: The official library for integrating Python with the MT5 terminal. It is the essential bridge that enables real-time data access and automated order execution.

    - Installation: pip install MetaTrader5

    - MetaTrader5 Documentation

- **pandas**: The primary tool for data manipulation. We use it to structure historical data into DataFrames, which simplifies the process of cleaning data and engineering features.

    - Installation: pip install pandas

    - pandas Documentation

- **numpy**: A fundamental package for scientific computing, providing support for efficient numerical operations on our data arrays.

    - Installation: pip install numpy

    - NumPy Documentation

- **scikit-learn (sklearn)**: The cornerstone of our machine learning pipeline. It provides the tools for nearly every stage of our process, including train_test_split, StandardScaler, Pipeline, GridSearchCV, and the classifiers themselves.

    - Installation: pip install scikit-learn

    - scikit-learn Documentation

- **imblearn (imbalanced-learn)**: A crucial library for addressing class imbalance in our training data. We use its SMOTETomek implementation to create a more balanced dataset for the model to learn from.

- o Installation: pip install imbalanced-learn

- o imbalanced-learn Documentation

- **pandas-ta**: This technical analysis library is essential for ensuring consistency in feature calculation between our historical data preparation and our live trading bot.

  - o Installation: pip install pandas_ta

  - o pandas-ta Documentation

- **seaborn & matplotlib**: These are our primary visualization libraries, used to generate the informative PnL charts and other statistical graphics in our backtesting analysis.

  - o Installation: pip install seaborn matplotlib

A.2 MetaTrader 5 Setup

MT5 is the trading platform that acts as the gateway to the market for our Python script.

1. **Download and Install MetaTrader 5:**

   - o Visit the official MetaTrader 5 website to download and install the platform.

2. **Set Up a Demo or Live Trading Account:**

   - o Create an account with a broker that supports MT5. It is strongly recommended to begin with a **Demo Account** for all testing and development.

   - o Log in to your account through the MT5 terminal.

3. **Enable Python Integration:**

   - o In the MT5 terminal, go to Tools -> Options -> Expert Advisors.

   - o Check the box for "Allow algorithmic trading".

4. **Connecting Python to MT5:**

   - o Ensure the MT5 terminal is running and you are logged in.

   - o Use the following Python commands at the start of your script to initialize the connection:

Acknowledgments

Writing this book has been an incredible journey, one filled with challenges, insights, and breakthroughs that could never have been achieved alone. It would not have been possible without the love, support, and inspiration from many individuals and communities who have shaped both the process and the final product. I owe a great debt of gratitude to all those who contributed—whether knowingly or unknowingly—to this work.

First and foremost, I want to express my deepest thanks to my God YHWH, my heavenly Father, whose wisdom, grace, and guidance have been my source of strength and clarity throughout this entire journey.

To my beloved mother, María del Socorro, thank you for being my constant pillar of support. Your unwavering belief in me, even when the process seemed endless, was a profound source of motivation. To my entire family, thank you for your continuous encouragement. Your faith in my work kept me focused during the most challenging moments. Every word and every line of code in this book is infused with the love and support I received from each of you.

A profound thanks is also due to the global open-source community—you are the unsung heroes and digital architects of modern innovation. The remarkable individuals who develop and maintain libraries like **pandas**, **scikit-learn**, **NumPy**, **pandas-ta**, **imblearn**, and **XGBoost** have provided the essential tools that allowed this project to exist. Your commitment to open collaboration and knowledge sharing has democratized technology, making it possible for researchers everywhere to explore complex frontiers like algorithmic trading. This book would not exist without the powerful ecosystem you have built.

I also want to express my deep appreciation to the trading and data science communities that thrive online across forums, blogs, and social media. Your collective wisdom, shared insights, and tireless contributions have served as guiding stars. Special thanks to the members of various MetaTrader forums, where countless discussions have sparked ideas and provided solutions that helped refine the practical trading strategies included in this text. Your openness and willingness to share what you've learned have shaped this book in profound ways.

To the readers of this book, I extend my heartfelt gratitude. Whether you are a seasoned trader, a data scientist, or someone embarking on your first steps into machine learning, thank you for choosing to invest your time in this work. It is my deepest hope that the concepts, methods, and strategies within these pages serve as a valuable and robust foundation for your own journey. Your curiosity and passion are what give this book life and relevance.

Finally, I want to extend my gratitude to everyone who has acted as a mentor, collaborator, or source of inspiration. Whether through direct conversations, shared knowledge, or simply by being an example of excellence, your impact has been felt throughout this entire process. Every chapter is, in some way, a reflection of your contributions, and for that, I am deeply thankful.

This book has been a labor of love, born from a desire to push boundaries, challenge conventional wisdom, and explore the powerful intersection of data, technology, and financial markets. I am excited to see how the ideas presented here will evolve in your hands.

To everyone who has walked this path with me, thank you. This work is dedicated to you and to the continuous pursuit of knowledge, growth, and success.

Happy trading, and may your journey be as rewarding and transformative as mine has been.